Poor Artists

Poor Artists

Gabrielle de la Puente
and Zarina Muhammad
(aka The White Pube)

PRESTEL

Munich • London • New York

First published in 2024 by Particular Books, an imprint of Penguin Press.
Penguin Press is part of the Penguin Random House group of companies,
whose addresses can be found at global.penguinrandomhouse.com.

US edition © Prestel Verlag, Munich · London · New York, 2024
A member of Penguin Random House Verlagsgruppe GmbH
Neumarkter Strasse 28 · 81673 Munich

A Library of Congress Control Number is available.

A CIP catalogue record for this book is available from the British Library.

Editorial direction: Ali Gitlow
Production management: Luisa Klose
Printing and binding: GGP Media GmbH, Pößneck

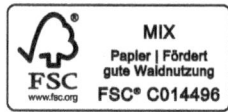

Penguin Random House Verlagsgruppe FSC® N001967

Printed in Germany

ISBN 978-3-7913-8021-6

www.prestel.com

Contents

Foreword

This book has been written by 90,000 people or there-
abouts. We lost count.

The first two writers are us: Gabrielle de la Puente
and Zarina Muhammad. Born seven days apart in
Liverpool and London, we met in art school where we
entered as painters and left as critics. It turned out
we enjoyed talking about art more than making it. We
enjoyed talking about art more than reading about it too.
We didn't get on well with the essays by dead French
men, or the non-committal newspaper reviews. Tutors
would order us to subscribe to expensive art magazines
and the more we think about it, the more we're convinced they were working on commission.

One afternoon when we were busy doing nothing in the
studio, we joked that we should start our own art
criticism website. *What should we call it?* Gabrielle
asked. *The White Pube!* Zarina screamed, and that one
joke changed the course of our lives. The name simul-
taneously took the piss out of the White Cube gallery
format, the international gallery chain, white supremacy,
the old guard and professionalism. Gabrielle bought the
domain name and that was that. Since 2015, we have
been posting weekly reviews on exhibitions, games,
films, books, restaurants, theme parks and a friend's

wedding. We take turns writing about whatever gets on our nerves for better or for worse, and try to write with accents, chests and guts. We work as part-time critics now, and we can't really believe that Zarina's joke has led us all the way to a book.

The next twenty-two writers are people we interviewed during the research phase of *Poor Artists*. During our time as critics, we have often zoomed out from individual pieces of art to think about the creative industry that artworks and artists have to contend with. It's not easy to be an artist. It's not easy to secure yourself a life in which you get to do the creative thing that gives you a reason to live, and yet art gets made *anyway*. This book is about the *anyway*. We spoke with artists, curators, technicians, teachers and museum directors. We spoke to a Turner Prize-winner or two, a Venice Biennale fraudster, a communist messiah, a few ghosts and a literal knight. We wanted to know the strategies people put in place to hold on to their relationship with art. With their support, the contents of those anonymous interviews informed some of the dialogue, metaphors and general narrative panic in the story we went on to write – a story made much richer for including perspectives beyond our own, from people who were able to be honest, ashamed, generous and truly critical in their anonymity.

The other 89,976-odd writers come from the international readership we have accumulated. Our sense of the art world has been shaped in part by the endless conversation we have been having online since this very serious joke began back in 2015, and, honestly, we don't go outside much, so thank you for letting us know how bad it really is on the ground.

Poor Artists blends fact and fiction. We see it as a series of interviews with ourselves and other people, told as a story. The book is full of composite characters who present an exquisite corpse portrait of what it means to work in contemporary art. *And* art history, because we did also speak to ghosts, remember? These are not rational events, and even though you are reading a piece of art criticism that might well have come from the non-fiction section, it is important that you let go of any expectations of rationality. The book features cannibal gallerists, a talking mountain and a terrible man called the Art King, and it's up to you how much you're willing to believe is real.

Warning

I'm dying. Or this is a panic attack. I thought panic attacks meant breathing fast and sweating profusely, not shitting fast and feeling existential on a plane toilet. Listen, the next twenty-nine chapters might be overwhelming, but I need you to feel how overwhelmed I felt when all of this real stuff really happened to me.[1]

It's my own fault. I'm lying about my identity. My name is Quest Talukdar, but the gallery paying for this flight to an art fair in LA is under the impression I am April Furst, assistant to the emerging artist QT. I am all three of these people, hence the business-class panic attack. They think I'm hand-delivering them an exclusive new painting for QT's booth at Frieze Art Fair, a classy shindig where rich people buy neon lights for more money than my Nani ever made in her entire life. I cannot look this anxious as a brown person on a flight. I need to come to my senses. I need my tummy to stop

---

1. Speaking of overwhelming, there are going to be a lot of footnotes to back up this story. You can ignore every single one of them and not miss out. You just might gain something if you do look into them. Maybe you'll feel like you're gaining enough by reading the main body of text, in which case, fuck the footnotes, but we'll include them in case you are in the mood, or in need.

1

hurting. I need people to believe the reason I'm panicking is not because I have a bomb on me but because
my desperation to become an artist has sent me off the
narrative deep end. This is what art has done to my
poor body. This is what art has been doing since
act one.

Lemon

I am literally a baby. Soft, chubby cheeks, big moon eyes. There is a bangle on my wrist; the gold disappears into a fold on my fat brown arm. Matching studs in my ears, hair all over the place. I need baby hair gel, but I'm not sure Mum knows it exists.

I'm only wearing one sock. When Mum cottons on, she is going to have to backtrack through the entire museum until she finds it. By that point, I will have kicked the other one off. If I could speak, I would let her know that I am getting ready to experience these weird dusty rooms, rooms where a surprising number of people keep gathering to just . . . *look* at stuff. Including us. Mum wrestles the pram on to the bus and gets off on the waterfront to begin our tour through The Museums. There is a people museum, a boat one, an animal one, but I like the picture museum best – and there is no point coming to The Museums if I can't feel the glossy wood under my feet when Mum finally lets me loose from the pram. I want my Experience!

Have you been to an exhibition before? You should go, I reckon. They can be kind of insane. I overheard Mum telling her friend that they're the only time I stop crying. She's right, to be fair. My baby brain is too busy processing what I am seeing and feeling. I think everyone should try them, especially if they have trouble controlling their emotions like I do. I never know what is going to happen inside an exhibition, and that's what makes it such a good training ground for the rest of my life.

If you're not familiar, exhibitions are special rooms with special things inside them. There are things that resemble other things and other-other things that look like nothing at all. The rooms can be great big halls, normal rooms like the ones in your house, or tiny places with random things crammed in. You have to pull a Goldilocks to decide which kind you like best. There are cosy wooden rooms that are often full of grandparents, and less cosy ones painted white. Not as many people go to the exhibitions in white rooms; the floor is concrete, and it's a bloody nightmare when you've got no socks on.

Exhibitions usually consist of pictures stuck on the walls. I didn't know why, or how. Maybe Blu Tack? I've also seen quite a few tellies in exhibitions. They are never playing anything I recognize, but if you watch for long enough, the programme eventually loops back to the start. If you liked it the first time around, you can watch it ten more times – or however high you can count.

Sometimes it's not even pictures or tellies filling the rooms, but humans are the things on display. I've seen grown-ups doing some weird dances. They're *very* serious when they go about it. Usually donning adult Babygros, they move in slow motion while ignoring my constant waves. I *have* to specify humans when I talk about the exhibition dancers because I've seen chickens and butterflies performing in galleries too. Except, I don't think the animals had rehearsed because they weren't very good.

No, you never know. Exhibitions are a pass-the-parcel surprise. Sometimes Mum and I roll in and there isn't anything to see, only strange sounds for us to listen to, sounds that seem to rearrange the atmosphere. The mad thing is that rearrangement never ends. We once went into a room to find a car crash, but for some reason the car wasn't on the road where cars go, it was on the top floor of the museum. We went back another time and the crash was gone. Instead, the room was a beach. Mum didn't comment on it, but I was speechless because, quite frankly, it was the biggest peekaboo I'd seen anyone pull off to date.

In the randomized dream of the exhibition space, Mum has carried me through pastel-coloured fog, and towards a burning sun. We've walked under black rain that stopped as soon as we approached. How did they coax the weather inside like that? I am desperate to know. I get the sense the rules are different inside museums. I've seen walls covered in blue crystals, and really strong lights in the shape of alphabetti spaghetti. We once walked into a room that you had to hum to get into, and that's when I learnt how to hum. We had to queue for a very long time to get into a dark box full of pumpkins and mirrors, all so that Mum could take a picture of us on her phone. We queued a separate time to bump around inside a room that had been filled with balloons. Everyone was taking pictures inside there as well. The static really aggravated my look, but Mum still didn't give me any hair gel. She has no shame.

When we are ready to go home, Mum plonks me back in my pram and we exit through the gift shop. One time, there was a playground slide attached to an upstairs window and the visitors were pumped out of the side of the building. I screamed, and then I stopped screaming and laughed. I wanted to go again right away, but I was fighting sleep. It really takes it out of me to do all of this experiencing. That must be the other reason Mum brings me to The Museums. By the time we leave, I am always out like a light.

Mum said that this stuff is what people call Art. It lives in museums, galleries and fancy homes. It can be outside in the wild. There is a big sharp silver line sticking out of a roundabout near our house, and Mum says that is Art too. I remember when we went into town and the whole of Liverpool had been taken over by colourful sculptures of animals. They were yellow lambs with sharp, curvy tails. Mum leant over the pram and said that the lambananas were Art as well. Did she say 'lambanana'? It is hard enough making the *baa* sound when an adult points at a sheep; what the fuck is a genetically modified banana supposed to sound like?

I enjoy being a baby, but it can't half get confusing. There is a lot to catch up on. In her live bedtime lecture series on the story of Art, Mum explained that there were certain people responsible for these fruit-animal hybrids. They were called *artists*. She said these people, *artists*, made stuff up in their heads and then later made them with their hands. They shared their art in dedicated exhibition rooms, and on roundabouts, so that other people got to see inside their heads.

And that's all well and good, but Mum delivers this information as if it is the most normal thing in the world. She takes me to museums like they are standard days out, but exhibitions are a changing, alien landscape. I *know* Tesco. Tesco has food. I know the zoo. Not a single lambanana in sight. In the gallery, I don't know what is going on. I know I am enjoying myself, but I am big enough to admit that I am absolutely lost for words. I don't know if there is something I should be *doing*? I feel like a bit of a melt just sitting there, you know? For all Mum's wisdom, she has never actually told me what to do. I have had to figure that one out on my own.

I have learnt to make sense of the art by making sense of myself.

I was sitting in a greasy plastic high chair in the museum café where Mum often meets her friend for carrot cake. Disgusting. There were no other babies to do baby-telepathy with so I made sure to do a really annoying cry to let Mum know I wanted to go back upstairs. She didn't budge. Instead, she placed a wet yellow thing on the tray in front of me. Mum and her friend both had their phones out. I didn't know why. I forgot my audience and grabbed whatever it was. I pushed it between my gums and I – I knew right away that she had poisoned me. My tongue got hot. My face started squeezing itself into a smaller face. Big dribbles. Really big dribbles. If the adults were laughing, I couldn't tell because my eyes were full of tears. As soon as they put their phones away, something took over. I decided to put the hot-yellow-poison straight back into my mouth.

I felt rabid. Genuinely elated. I felt this good, mad rush because I couldn't decide if I loved or hated this thing. I had to taste it over and over again to find out. I was squirming in my seat, dancing, tears rolling down my cheeks. A third time, a fourth, just to be sure. The conclusion was: I hated it. But I loved the experience that contained such hate. Discovering something new was giving me a thrill for being alive in a body, all meat and bones, with these opinions bursting out of me.

Mum cleaned me up, and on returning to the gallery, I realized that I could go about art in the same way. When I am in an exhibition, I am a baby trying a lemon for the

8

first time. I place the art on the sticky plastic tray in front of me, consume it, and then await my own reaction. It's a game I play, an experiment; a way to feel less lost in the exhibition by following the lead of my feelings. This reaction is slippy. It might bubble out of my conscience, or come out of my heart. It can land anywhere on my body or nowhere, depending on the art and me. It might make me laugh out loud. It might make me feel warm. It might be a vague flavour, something to mull over. Or it might sting. I can get angry and distressed; spit the art back out, or swallow it fast like medicine. I can get a shock, a stomach drop. I might find an artwork that's harder to parse, a feeling I've never felt before. Each discovery leads to an expansion.

Art is only a picture on a wall, but I am there getting clammy in my pram. A painting reminds me of something scary, and I have to close my eyes. A statue shows me who I want to be, and I stare. Once I know what face the art has made me pull, it is up to me to decipher my nervous system's response. Like, OK, I can't look the painting in the eye because it reminds me of the clown at the fair. The fear is a clue towards shame because really I wish I was braver. See that statue over there – that one has always been easy to love, and my love for it easy to understand, because the statue looks exactly like Mum (Mum is really muscly).

I leave the art messy on the tray, examined; art leaves me messy in the seat, transformed. How can an exhibition do this to me, even for a moment? Who am I now the experience is over? I trace a line from the artworks to each of these questions, and it is tricky, like a dot-to-dot puzzle I scribble over with my wobbly baby hands. I am proud when the connections reveal a new hidden picture between the constellation of art and myself. It is how I began building a conscience, and it makes me believe a gallery is the very best place I could grow up in.

Mum takes us all over, but on Tuesday mornings, we go to the big museum by the river where there is a regular playdate for kids. The pictures are hung really low on the walls so we can crawl right up to them. There are lots of buttons with sound effects to press, and a wavy mirror that makes my head look even bigger. There are costumes, puppets and – I don't know what else, because the adults drop us in a circular soft-play area and we don't have the upper-body strength to climb back out.

The other babies are all right. A few like art, but most aren't fussed. Those ones must have been sick of me because every Tuesday morning I would try to tell them about the revelation of The Exhibition. Better than CBeebies, I'd tell them. Better than YouTube. I'd ask how everybody felt about lemons, and they'd tell me they weren't on solids yet, so I'd vaguely stand up and say: 'I go to exhibitions and my senses get pulled in opposite directions; my sense of self becomes a work in progress under the tension.'

I'd babble: 'If I can use big words for a moment, I think it is fascinating to witness a roll-of-the-dice aesthetic experience become a somatic event inside of me. It's destabilizing, like when Mum throws me up into the air – that split second before gravity remembers I'm there – I hope the art will catch me.'

Nothing.

'I like to imagine exhibitions are where we all go to change.'

I'd continue: 'The artist offers us something. What do *we* offer back? Is the exhibition a conversation? Maybe artists are talking to us. Whispering and singing and telling secrets and making very important speeches like this one.'

One of the regulars threw a toy at my head. I'd insist: 'When I experience art, I feel as though I am supposed to reply. It might be time I learnt how to speak. But I get the feeling I shouldn't reply with any exact language, though. When I grow up, I should make my own art so that I can speak back.'

I think I'm going to have to be an artist. I should practise my drawing. We have crayons at home, and I've been getting this real urge to draw on the walls of the living room lately. I should lean into that.

God, artists are the luckiest people alive! They get to have ideas for a living. The artists honoured in the museum are so lucky. Being an artist must be a really

important role that the whole world takes very seriously. So seriously that they build convoluted houses
to keep art safe. If art lives in palaces, I wonder where
artists rest their heads at night. Ha! I am so excited to
find out!

Phrogging

The creaking over my head was distracting at first. I kept having intrusive thoughts about the new tenant breaking through and squashing me. I had to keep reminding myself that I never got the sense the ground was going to give way when I was living up there – not the floorboards, anyway. Only then could I start to relax. Learn the lie of my new miniature land, the directions of the pipes. Arrange a home for myself: a bed in the insulation, a giant pet mouse and, of course, my own studio.

Mum would have burst out laughing if she could have seen me, except she'd have had to squint through a gap in the floorboards. I never told her what happened. Not Mum or the aunties. As good as it felt to have so much space, I also had a lot of shame. Everyone expected me to move straight back home after art school. They kept going on about how London was too expensive, *especially for an artist.* I didn't disagree, but the way they said it made me want to prove them wrong. It made me want to cling to London for dear life. Because, for better or worse, I was convinced that it was a place where enough creative things were happening that if I hung around for long enough, I was bound to get swept up by one of them.

Maybe the sweeping would occur on First Thursdays, when galleries in the east held late-night openings, and there were drinks and music, and the tourists filling the streets were replaced with hundreds of artists in thrifted outfits. Or maybe I'd make an impression at an intersectional reading group, where intense people competed to prove their intensity; where I might say something that was poignant and new and political, but not problematic to anyone, anywhere, at any time throughout history. Maybe on a silent walk, at an artist's talk, a book launch or a life-drawing class – the kind that happened in cafés after hours, where well-moisturized women wore linen and drank herbal tea. I didn't know how to communicate this London-specificity to my aunties. They didn't quite realize how long I was willing to wait to become a part of the art world. But I did. It was for ever.

When I first told my family I wanted to study art, they held a really shit intervention. The aunties said that artists only make money when they're dead. Nani put a hand on top of mine and said that I was a smart girl. I shouldn't waste my talents. I should do something with numbers. With money. I could get a nice house, a nice car, and then a nice man would want to marry me. Once I'd had his many, many babies, I could paint to my heart's content. I was only sixteen – she'd had two kids by my age.

Nani nudged my uncle, who'd been quiet the whole time; I'd spent the summer scanning family photographs on his orders. He'd given me fifty quid because he didn't know how computers worked, and this man – who knew my plans to cut a one-inch fringe and buy a jarg[2] Fjällräven bag off eBay with my summer earnings – had the cheek to say: 'Quest's next job could be in cyber. She just doesn't know it yet.'

Mum flipped. She said Nana would be rolling in his grave if he could hear the way they were carrying on.

'Nana didn't come to this country for us to live a small life that other people decided for us. The whole point was for us to have choices.'

She went on about how it can't only be rich kids who get to have exhibitions or the world would end. South Asian kids can't all be lawyers or doctors or account-ants or, God forbid, politicians. (She neglected to mention I didn't actually have the grades to do any of those things.) She said that if I did any random subject at university other than art, I'd end up dropping out due to sheer misery. That shut them up because, really, all they wanted was someone in the family to finally have a degree. I'd never seen his work, but I reminded them Nana used to tell me all the time that he was an artist; Nani looked at the floor and said that's because he was always drawing the dole.

2. 'Jarg' is a word used colloquially in Liverpool to mean 'fake', specifically a knock-off branded item.

It would have been more sensible to study something like *cyber*, they were right. The house opposite got shot at last year, my 'Dad' is AWOL, Mum's a dinner lady and unfortunately kids don't tip. But I thought everything would work itself out. I'd get maximum student loans. I'd try really hard. I'd sell all the paintings I'd eventually make for the degree show[3] – and then when the bill came at the end of my graduation dinner, to celebrate my First Class BA (Hons), I'd humbly pay for everyone and they'd finally respect my chosen field because I'd have gallery representation and get nominated for the Turner Prize or something.

None of that happened, obviously. I ended up making very uncommercial sculptures and getting a 2:1. There was no fancy dinner because the price of train tickets in this country means that Nani can't fucking see the country she lives in beyond the view out of her own front windows – the drive-by shootings, the year-round fireworks, the police wandering around aimlessly because no one will tell them shit.

University was over with, and I was hanging around London like Billy-no-mates, and sort of instantly depressed having reckoned with the amount of debt I was in. It was £47,701 on graduating, a number that didn't seem real or mine, rising to £57,823 a mere six

3. University degrees in Fine Art typically culminate in an exhibition of students' work called a degree show.

years later due to 'interest'.[4] Money is all I could think about. I think maybe it's all I've ever thought about. Art first, money a close second. I was simply terrified once I realized that there was a cost to living. Doesn't seem right, does it? Not one of us asked to be born. Doesn't seem right that the poorest students leave with the most debt.

Max

Does anyone wanna come and see Apichatpong Weerasethakul's new film at Tate Modern on Saturday?

Quest

i'll pass

Quest

going outside means £travel plus £tickets if we go to whatever's on upstairs at Tate, £food and £drink if we stay out too long, and then £travel home and my £rent is already £too £much

---

4. Gabrielle de la Puente's real student finance figures on graduating from Central Saint Martins in 2016.

Yelena

Yeah, I can't do a day out either

Max

The screening is free btw

Yelena

London is not

> **Quest**
>
> i've been trying to find somewhere new to live and I keep coming across listings for rooms you can ONLY rent during the weekdays or ONLY rent between 5pm and 9am

Yelena

life is hell on Earth

Max

wait are you moving?

> **Quest**
>
> the rent is going up again

> **Quest**
>
> also i was trying to do an art shift after a work shift and i got

expanding foam on the floor and
i had to go at it with a hammer
and there were blue chips flying
everywhere and the security
deposit flashed before my eyes

Quest
and it's just shit because none of
this would happen if i had a
studio

A studio is a space where artists can make a mess
without consequence, or where mess is only a consequence of research. It is space where art can stay a work
in progress, and art is allowed to settle. However ugly or
precarious or unbalanced the uncooked work is, the
artist can come back the next day to see what needs to
change. If I mix a certain colour of paint but have to
wash the palette because there's nowhere to leave
it – because this 'studio' is also my bedroom, dining
room, living room and wardrobe – then there's no
guarantee I'll be able to achieve that exact shade a
second time.

Yelena

do you not wanna fork out a third of your wages for a *clean co-working space* where no one speaks to each other and everyone has their meetings without headphones and you definitely can't whip out some paintbrushes?

Quest

i wish i was a graphic designer

Yelena

I hear they make actual money. People *pay* them

Quest

i don't believe it

Yelena

every inch of this city is monetized. People with cars have to pay for the three metres of road outside their house just to park

Yelena

thank god we can't drive

Quest

thank god

Quest

the other day i unravelled some
unstretched canvas I'd left
under the window and it was
pure mould inside

Yelena

the world's worst Swiss roll

Max

It's ridiculous, this ruse of a worldview – that
floors and walls and air and a door could cost
so much

Quest

ridiculous that other
professions have purpose-
built workplaces that they get
paid to go to, and artists have
nowhere AND no one paying
them to go there

Max

I think because art is a hobby for some people, the
rest of the population can't seem to respect that it is
actually a job

Max

Adults look at artists and think, you do that thing we all did when we were kids – the scribbling and drawing and finger-painting – I wish I had kept doing that too. But because they didn't, they infantilize it

Yelena

we need a uniform

Quest

there are enough dickheads in blue workers jackets if we want to go with those[5]

Quest

i just know that if I never have a studio, i'll never be able to THINK

---

5. An anthropological explanation: middle-class men in art love to co-opt the historically working-class garment *le bleu de travail*. The bright blue utilitarian jacket was originally worn by French railway workers. These modern men in urbane environs don't actually do any manual labour, nor are they exposed to the elements. They want to look capable, but they are only capable of smooth jazz playlists and mansplaining aperture. Give the French their jackets back!

Quest

my phone is gonna have to be
my studio, camera roll archive
and moodboard, Notes app
journal, Group chat crits.[6]
Who's in????

Yelena

that makes me feel even more claustrophobic than
I already am

Yelena almost moved back to Manchester after university, but rent was getting as bad up there as it was down
here. So, she got a studio in a massive building near the
Isle of Dogs, nailed down some 8 × 4s, and built herself
a storage space halfway up the walls (except the
storage was actually for her). She left her flat behind
so she was only paying one lot of rent, and she told
me she's heard things at night – she thinks other people
are secretly living there too. She also said she's never
made so much art in her life. On the other hand, she
wees in a bucket after dark so security don't catch on,
and she may or may not have regular nightmares about
the night guard finding her. But that's not a good

6. There is a whole chapter coming up on group crits, but if you want
the TL;DR now, a group crit is when a bunch of artists get together
and discuss the work they are making with the aim of giving the maker
feedback and direction.

enough reason to leave, is it, when there are more important reasons to stay.

Yelena

Phrogging is a form of protest.[7] Phrogging is a way to undermine the rentier class.[8]

I thought a lot about how she wasn't actually *allowed* to sleep in her studio because *planning permission* determines what buildings can and cannot be used for. Studios are for work, not sleep, because *someone* at *the council* is a *bore*. When she told me what she was doing, I felt like that annoying person who suddenly realizes *we live in a society.* But we do! And I don't like it! Because even when someone accesses space, somebody else's rules determine how they behave inside of it. Can't be sleeping in a studio. Can't be holed up panicking inside the toilet on board a Boeing 747 for the entire flight. People just make these rules up. The plane is massive. There are bathrooms everywhere.

7. If you look up 'phrogging', loads of scary true-crime stories appear about people secretly living in the walls and attics of other people's homes. Exciting.

8. Rentiers are people who earn money from capital without having to lift a finger. For example, evil landlords.

Fuck the privatization of the toilet. Fuck the privatization of the sky.[9]

The art I made in my horrible shared flat got smaller and smaller until it was gone, and when I stopped making art, I stopped feeling like myself. I followed Yelena's lead and I didn't renew my tenancy. Instead I just . . . let it happen. The smaller I was made to feel, the bigger the world around me became. Eventually, I fell down a crack in the floor, and that's where I've stayed. Yeah, there was a twinge of shame. But I remember the relief so fondly. I thought, if this much square footage was scaled up and put on the market, it would turn into a Westfield, Boxpark,[10] or maybe Secret Cinema[11] would nab it. I stopped thinking about the privatization of planet Earth because I had moved on; I used the end of a pin to carve shapes into a rubber armature that I repurposed from a bobble I'd dropped down here ages ago. Every day, I would carve until my tiny hands got tired. To this day, it's still the best work I've ever made.

9. I guess the studio rule is because firefighters need to know where people are in the event of an emergency. But houses burn down all the time, and I'd much rather die in my studio (if I had one). (God, I think about death a lot. It goes art first, money second, and then popping my clogs.)

10. London is covered in these shipping-container-turned-pop-up-shop venues where a single pint costs £10 and all the burgers are covered in truffle oil.

11. An immersive film company, established in 2007.

Max

I wish I could phrog.

I ignored the chorus of aunties beckoning me back home over the years because even though it might be more comfortable to live above the floors, I didn't want to be under their roof and their rules. It's like what happened to Max. His mum set him up in the garden shed. Strong start. At university, Max used to spend weeks layering oil paint on canvas until the paint was almost as thick as the support. He was obsessed with trying to do an Alexis Harding – the heavy, kinetic trickery of getting the paint to slide off when he finally hung the piece upright on a wall. The tutors were as obsessed with Max as he was with Harding. They said he was *going places*. Unfortunately he'd gone to a shed in Leicestershire – a shed his mum proceeded to knock on *all day long* to check in. She meant well, but the sound of knocking created a Pavlovian response of the deepest frustration.

Max then got an email from a gallery in town asking for a studio visit. He wasn't keen on inviting a curator into his tight-knit situation, but it wasn't as if curators were getting in touch every day, so he squeezed an extra chair in. He was nervous. He said he caught himself spraying aftershave like he would before a date, which made sense; the gallery was looking for graduates who they could establish *long-term working relationships* with. If it went well, it might lead to a second date and maybe back to their place for an exhibition. The meeting went fairly well until Max's Mum *and* Dad knocked on the door of the shed five minutes in and never left. They told the curator to show Max's work at the gallery. But also Monet. *A nice Monet exhibition. We'd go to that, wouldn't we? And who's the lad who did the shiny babies – the radiant babies. Keith Haring. Do him after that.* Max never got to speak about his own work, and, funnily enough, he never heard back.

I didn't tell my friends or family what had happened when I fell under the floor. I didn't have the words to talk about it at that point, only the *sense* that I wanted to live every day with art and only art in mind like a superfan, devotee, groupie or professional hermit. Besides, I struggled to admit this wish because I needed it to sound serious, and it never did. When the aunties used to ask me to move back, and when they'd tell me about jobs going, they were prodding at a very specific vulnerability. I was convinced they saw 'Artist' as a pipe dream I could let go of when push came to shove, and not a career I was dedicated to. They seemed to think Artist sat outside the remit of a *proper adult life.* I couldn't tell them I would rather reject student debt, landlordism,[12] building regulations, reality and all the

---

12. Freee Art Collective (Mel Jordan, Andrew Hewitt and Dave Beech) released a series of slogan scarves in 2017. One of them said, 'There is no housing shortage, only the monopoly of property. Postlandlord-ism.' Gabrielle de la Puente wears it every winter. Gabrielle de la Puente uses it to wipe her tears.

other gross-up close-up activities that adults are so preoccupied with. I couldn't tell them because I didn't want to criticize them for accepting society as it is; I'd be saying, I want *this* life because I certainly don't want *yours*. Your life is full of interruptions that get in the way of making art, and I'd prefer peace and quiet and a freedom that I might only gain in some radical infant-ilized state – in privacy, secrecy, fiction and play. All I want is to be an artist. But that's too much to ask.

Studio Time

In the 2023 diptych by Mollie Balshaw, the artist upholstered two vertical frames with the Stagecoach bus
company's signature moquette, the frantic blue-and-
orange-patterned fabric that is supposed to distract
from graffiti and stains. Balshaw then used acrylic paint
to scrawl the words *MY STUDIO IS ON THE BUS*
across the two bus seats. A recognition of the artistic
design the public experiences as part of everyday life,
the work also admits that art is something working-
class artists must squeeze in between other jobs
whenever, wherever and however they can.

In 2002, the Portuguese artist João Onofre set a vulture
loose in his studio. In the nine-minute video he
captured, the animal pecks at the papers Onofre has
stuck up across the wall, knocks books off his shelves
and flies awkwardly back and forth across the confined
space making loud, agitated sounds. The resulting
video shows a symbol of death and destruction
becoming a reality in a space known for artistic production. A wild animal disoriented by the small studio where
wild artists orient themselves and their ideas.

In Ghislaine Leung's exhibition for the 2023 Turner Prize,
one wall inside the Towner Gallery in Eastbourne was
painted with a thin grid. The dimensions of the grid

matched the wall that the artist uses in her studio at home, and it was divided into twenty-four sections and seven rows to indicate the hours in a week. A section towards the centre of the grid was filled in with black paint to represent the time Leung is able to spend in her studio, between 9 a.m. and 4 p.m. on Thursdays and Fridays. The piece, titled *Hours*, shows how little time artists are able to claim – even *successful* artists nominated for the most prestigious art prizes in the UK.

When unemployment meant that Dawn Kasper had to give up her studio, the artist made a proposal to the Whitney Biennial in 2012 that she would bring her workplace into the New York museum and practise in view of the public during their opening hours. The artist made music and collage, drew pictures, read books, worked on her laptop, and hosted audiences in impromptu studio visits. Illuminating the day-to-day activity of an artist's responsibilities, the project not only gave Kasper a studio to work in but it also provided her with employment for the duration of the festival – and then again in 2017, when she toured the work to the Venice Biennale for a six-month performance.

In 1999, Tracey Moffatt and Gary Hillberg montaged representations of art in film and television. Beginning calmly in the studio, the video shows artists painting portraits and chiselling sculptures, before we see a monkey painting in a smock. Footage cycles through conversations about investing in art, how bad it is, and how many artists regret their life choices, or are simply full of anger. Shirley MacLaine shoots a canvas with an automatic rifle; and there is a heated scene in which one artist shouts, 'All I see when I look at your painting is that you paint too fast!' before the other screams, 'You look too fast!' Stereotypes in popular media position artists as eccentric outcasts who should either be pitied, feared or laughed at.

Wendy

When I was a teenager, I used to stay at Nani's every Friday night with all of my cousins. We'd order a huge pizza and a very wide three-litre bottle of Coke. I'd eat my allotted slices as fast as possible, inhale caffeine and head to the kitchen alone. I had art to attend to. While everyone else watched the wrestling, I'd be sat at the dinner table squeezing paint across the reflective surface of the old steel thali Nani gave me to use as a palette – not the nice ones we used for special occasions like birthdays, iftar, the Derby, Eurovision, jummah mubarak or the Grand National. I didn't care. Friday nights were for painting with no bedtime.

I think that's when my life peaked. I'd paint anything. A sunset, a tree, the old tins of soup that had been in the cupboard since before I was born. Various cousins would come in and out of the kitchen and they'd ignore whatever I was working on to request portraits of Rey Mysterio. They wanted me to do a Michelangelo on the ceiling of Nani's living room, swapping heaven for a wrestling ring and half-naked angels for half-naked men in the throes of a Royal Rumble. They were being nice. I wasn't that good.

I didn't feel embarrassed about my skill. I had more grace for myself back then. I believed I had an innate passion for creative expression, and that belief was enough encouragement. Even if my attempt at The Undertaker jumping off the top rope looked nothing like the man, there was so much enjoyment to be had in the process of making an artwork. Art gave me the most amazing feeling. There was nothing like it. It felt *so* good, it made me want to *go in.*

Going in meant putting in the time. Mum said you had to sink 10,000 hours into something before you mastered it, which was tricky considering we were only set one period of Art each week in school. Hence the all-nighters. I had to clock my hours whenever I could; doodling in the margins of my homework, carving stars into the tables in class. The backs of my hands would always be covered in biro, despite the fact every teacher warned me about ink poisoning. I used to memorize quotes about art, and if they were small enough, I would write them on myself like temporary tattoos.

'The imaginative tool is in us all.'[13]

Clive Barker said that one. He wrote *Hellraiser* and *Candyman* (the cousins sometimes liked to scare me because I was the youngest). Barker was also from Liverpool, which excited me, and even though his stories gave me nightmares, I used to hunt down his

13. From an interview with Clive Barker on *The South Bank Show*, TV programme, episode broadcast 10 April 1994.

interviews because maybe it would give me clues on how to get to where he is now. In one of them, he said: 'My life has absolutely been transformed by the imaginative possibilities offered to me by artists. Isn't that one of the reasons why we go to books and paintings and theatre and movies? We go because we want our lives enriched and that enrichment is a kind of change. We want our pain illuminated, and if it's illuminated maybe it isn't quite so bad.'

That one didn't fit on the back of my hand, so I wrote it on the front of my school planner. It really put me at risk of becoming emo.

Going in meant learning the lingo. I used to watch BBC documentaries at the weekends and give the presenters more of my attention than I ever gave the ink-poisoning brigade. Art had its own language: 'trompe-l'oeil', 'chiaroscuro', 'hegemony', 'imprimatura', 'pentimento', 'bourgeois', 'impasto'. Was it 'gesso' or 'jesso'? And did 'sfumato' rhyme with the English 'tomato'?[14]

I liked *The World's Most Expensive Paintings*, but I liked the documentaries about famous fraudsters and art thieves even more. Also, *Simon Schama's Power of Art* series on Turner, Rothko and Bernini, amongst others. Nani said that ages ago, before I was born, you used to

14. Art language quiz. If you think you know the definitions, make a list and then turn to p. 288 for the answers. If you don't know them, they're there if you want to learn.

be able to post the BBC a cheque for £2.50 and they'd send you back an illustrated guide to accompany the show. A guide would have come in handy. I tried to keep a mental note of the stuff these artists used to make their work – if it didn't sound too medieval – and whenever we went to town, I'd go off on my own to look at the products in the art shops.

I hadn't realized there were so many types of pencils. Graphite came with a scale of hardness: hard, soft black, hard black and firm. That's why pencils have letters and numbers on the side; 8B is darker and smudgier than a light 2H. Rubbers too. Or maybe I should start saying erasers, because there are gum erasers, kneadable erasers, vinyl erasers and *rubber* erasers, and I can't go around calling them rubber rubbers. Did you know paper has *weight*? The thing you paint on is referred to as a 'support': paper, canvas, wood. You have to be careful with supports because certain ones need to be 'primed' before you apply the paint, otherwise it can chip off once it's done drying.

I would ask this woman in the art shop if she could tell me what the intimidating bottles on the shelves were for. She called them 'mediums'. Potions to mix in with paint so that it changes. I didn't understand what she meant, so she picked up a pot of crackle paste and told me it splits paint like dry skin. Artists use it to make an image look older than it actually is. Others reduced the likeli-hood of paintings yellowing over time, or they made paint dry faster or slower. Glossy or matt. She told me that one popular medium made oil paint act more like acrylic – it added a plastic consistency to the mix that made it easier to apply paint without leaving brush-marks behind. School wasn't set up for this degree of technical knowledge. Our art teacher hadn't even taught us there was more than one type of paint.

I could have listened to Art Shop Lady all day, and sometimes I did. She said that paint is pigment mixed with a binder. There are many combinations of chemicals that transform the way paint looks once it has dried; refracting light differently, and tweaking colour, consistency and intensity. Also affecting its cost. Poster paint was cheap. Watercolour, gouache, enamel, tempera and acrylic were a step up. There was emulsion for decorating inside, masonry paint for outside, spray paint for making outside more fun, and then there was oil paint, which made Art Shop Lady speak in hushed and reverent tones.

I was eyeing it up, filtering prices from low to high. I knew the big important artists in the documentaries used oils. But the ones she had in stock were seven quid a tube, and I couldn't get by on one colour, could I? I put the paint down and carried on with my education; she'd moved on to brushes. Synthetic or animal hair. Animal hair? *Hog bristle.* Well, I didn't like the sound of that. Hogs are pigs and pigs are haram. She told me about brush shapes next: round, angular, fan, stencil, wash. Then she said something about varnish. A thing you put on top of paintings to seal and protect them. A bit like the top coat my cousin Umaya uses when she's finished doing my nails. Yeah. To tint the image, she told me you could add a drop of pigment to the varnish – but I was only half-listening by that point. I'd had an idea, and the idea made me feel terrible. Honestly, this is where it all began.

I did see if the school could get some in, but the art teacher said the department didn't have an oil paint budget, or any budget, really. She said I'd have to go to a private school if I wanted that treatment, but I had other ideas. This circle of women used to knock round at Nani's on a Saturday to peddle their wares. I was quite impressed by these hunter-gatherers. They looked old and young at the same time, and they were called things like Wendy. They'd go round the shops in the afternoon when traffic was at its busiest, and come the evening, they'd pull brand-new lipsticks and steaks with security tags out of tiny handbags. Sunglasses, perfume, whatever they could get away with. Sometimes we'd have steak for dinner, but then we wouldn't see the Wendys for months at a time, and they'd say they'd been on their holidays.

I was usually silent during the haggling, but one night I asked Wendy if she ever got paint in.

'Paint, like, for the house? Babe, one of them's not gonna fit in here.'

I gave her the mission. I wanted oil paint, tiny tubes of the stuff. Multiple tubes if possible. I need ultramarine, which is blue. Titanium white. Ochre – that's a dirty yellow. Cadmium yellow, cadmium red as well. Burnt sienna, raw umber. Those are both brown and if you can get rose, which is –

'I already know what Rose looks like! She lives at the bottom of Warwick Street.'

I tried to join in with the laughter, but my stomach was on the floor. I wasn't going to be able to go back to the art shop and I went all the bloody time.

Going in meant *making art.* Laying out the elements. Gently patting colours, coaxing them together, light to dark. Changing the curve of a line, changing it back. Oil takes way longer to dry than the cheap stuff I was used to, and you can't mix oil paint with water, you need a thinner, and it is much easier to fix mistakes. To that end, time stopped being a limiting factor because I could always open the image like a portal. I'd stop noticing the cousins coming in and out of the kitchen. I had retreated to an interior mental landscape; a flow state in which the body's edges were dissolved.

Is it done? I would agonize. Stand back from the painting, go out of the room, come in again, look at the picture as if I was seeing it for the first time. I would pick it up, always getting paint on my fingertips, and take it upstairs to the landing so that I could look at it in the mirror. Now, I was someone else seeing it for the first time. If any of the cousins were still awake, I'd take it through to them, and if they looked surprised, I must have done all right. The cycle of creating a painting was so dramatic. Like, actually dramatic; I had to accept I was going to be unsettled through the first act, the second act and the crisis point – right up until the point when the hero saved the day.

'This is an art attack! This is an art attack! This. Is. *Art Attack*.'

I hadn't noticed the sun come up. CITV was playing reruns of the BAFTA award-winning kids' show for the Saturday-morning crowd. Neil Buchanan was bouncing around the screen – another Liverpool export. I watched that man religiously as a kid. Used to do the activities with Mum. Filling broken egg shells with watery paint and dropping them from up high so they made splats. Marbling paper, making invisible drawings with candle wax.

'Quest.'

I looked up at the screen.

'I have to laugh sometimes.'[15]

Did someone say my name?

'I go into an art shop to take a look round and the shelves are absolutely full of expensive, fancy art materials. Sometimes there are even people buying

15. Dialogue from *Best of Art Attack (2)*, TV episode, CITV, 1996.

39

hundreds of pounds worth of art equipment. Specialist paint, fancy brushes. Doesn't make you a better artist.'

He was looking directly at me.

'I think art's all about having fun. Being creative. Throwing away the rule books and doing your own thing, using anything you can lay your hands on. There's nothing wrong with that sort of stuff but you just don't need it. I mean, let's face it. We've created some really effective pieces of art together using the most unusual things.'

I'd seen enough *Art Attack* to know you didn't need the right materials to be an artist. What Neil didn't understand, however, is that *I wanted them.* Not needing them wasn't a good enough excuse to never have them, and not being able to afford them wasn't a good enough excuse either. The euphoria of creation surpassed every second of guilt I felt for my delin-quency. I know you shouldn't rob independent shops *now*, only Tesco. Looking back, maybe oil paint was my gateway into a life of crime. Maybe I did go on to peel the labels out of the back of the university library's books and flush microchips down the toilet so I could sneak them through the sensors with me, a free woman. Maybe I did nab a few postcards from gallery gift shops over the years. Who can say? Maybe I haven't paid for a gig ever since I learnt I could order wristbands in every colour online, rock up to a queue, see what colour the venue had gone with and waltz

40

in.[16] *Maybe* I took one of the fingernails from Cathy Wilkes' Turner Prize show and, because I'm not evil, chewed one of mine off to replace it. *Maybe* I pirate everything I watch like it's 2007 because when you go to a cinema, you have to watch pre-roll adverts for cars (irrelevant) or joining the army (brainwashing). *Maybe* I once took the Molton Brown hand soap out of the bathroom in the Victoria Miro Gallery because it smelt nice. *Maybe* I wanted to support the arts but couldn't afford to. Maybe I wanted the arts to support *me*. Nothing in the world mattered more to me than the way I felt about art, even when it seemed like it should, even when it compromised my princi—

'Quest!'

Neil?

'Bed!'

Not Neil, Nani. Ah shit.

16. In vlog 37 on American hardcore punk band Turnstile's YouTube channel, filmed on the occasion of their show at Ottobar in Baltimore, a fan talks about this wristband trick, and it's cool that Turnstile included the clip.

The Mountain

When I arrived at art school, my mind was still intact.
Not for long, though; the head of university was a pile
of leftover art. His name was Mark. I would stare every
time I walked around him in the studios – the novelty
never wore off. He used to be a man, according to the
rumours, but no one had been at the university long
enough to know for sure. All we had was the evidence
before us: Mark's body was a historical site of art and
materials; of canvas, plaster, cardboard and bubble
wrap. He couldn't move anywhere, but he did have
movement. Odd things stuck out of the mountain at
different times of the day as he adjusted against the
heft of himself. Poles appeared and disappeared.
Pipes, plinths, the edge of an easel. He was made up
of wood, empty paint cans, plastic sheeting, reconsti-
tuted foam – all the art student staples sloped up his
foothills. There was a giant mushroom made out of
bed sheets flowering behind his head, and a cliff of
mattresses running down his back, and he was
covered in a veneer of salt, sugar and crystalline
substances that made the mountain glitter under
skylights.

After handing in work for our final assessment, we came
to Mark one by one to give him the art we didn't want to

take with us when we left. Stuff that was too heavy or awkward to haul on public transport, and failed experiments that weren't destined to become art, so they became a part of Mark instead. He had two boxy black-and-white televisions for eyes – the old kind Nani once had, the *exact* kind early-career artists love because they're cheaper than flat screens and we think nostalgia matures us.

'Hello, child.'

I entered the studio dragging two heavy-duty bin bags behind me. Mark's mouth was a Lucio Fontana rip-off after a student had cut a slit in a stretched canvas, thinking the tutors wouldn't know where he'd got the idea from. The slice had a slight curl to it, making it look as though Mark was always smiling.

'What have you brought me?'

I couldn't decide what to grab out of the bin bags because it was all so embarrassing.

'But embarrassment is one of the most important qualities in art! Embarrassment is not confined to subject matter – yes, it's there when the extraordinary Icelandic artist Ragnar Kjartansson asks his mother to spit in his face for the sake of video art. But it's also there in the excruciating structure; when Ragnar and his dear actress mother reconvene every five years to film the next instalment, and their new spit is added on to the end of the old spitty film. Embarrassment grows! The blush deepens! Embarrassment is a texture we should always try to embellish our work with if we care about radical vulnerability. The more an artwork develops, the more polished we think it should become, but it's so much more interesting to let an artwork *be* embarrassing. That way it stays an un-generic, unprofessional, naive artefact of the self, unlike anything else. Embarrassment means an artwork is disarmed, and we can get up close and personal with it. We refer to Ragnar Kjartansson once more. In 2013, he invited moody American rock band The National to perform their song "Sorrow" repeatedly for a total of six hours on stage at a gallery in New York. The collaboration was, incidentally, called "A Lot of Sorrow", and the embarrassment quivered in the lyrics, of course. But it truly lived in the fatigue of the musicians' hands and their voices; in the deterioration of the audience; in the listener who hears the same words until they mean nothing at all. How excellent! I dare you to start with the most embarrassing thing you can find. I bet you I'm going to love it.'

One of our first lectures had made mention of Maria Lassnig. I wrote her name down and looked her up afterwards, and her work was like nothing I'd ever seen before. That sounds a bit over the top now that I know the many different forms art can take; she was only a painter, and there's loads of painters, and she painted people and things, and people and things are to be expected. But Maria Lassnig was new to me, and I was new to art school, where everybody was terrified of being criticized because criticism might lead to embarrassment. Here was Maria, naked and mad in unflattering poses. She had a frog on her crotch, a bloated guinea pig in her hand; one gun to her head and another aiming directly at the viewer.

It was funny. She was funny. Leaking her own nudes. She made neon colours look milky, and milky tones look neon. I ended up spending most of the year trying to match her palette, and I drove myself mad because I never got it right, not once.

Mark's canvas mouth smiled sympathetically.

'Lassnig was a great artist. But do you know why you drove yourself mad?'

His shoulder moved slowly and the tip of a traffic cone appeared.

'Because you were entering an *art degree*. It's different from every other discipline in that when you arrive on an undergraduate course, you're asked to create *new* knowledge. If you were somewhere else, doing a Maths degree for example, you wouldn't be required to create new knowledge until you got to PhD level. In Fine Art, you do it from the word go because it's your own practice that you're exploiting, developing and bringing to the fore. It's *your* art, *your* ideas. They're going to be new because you're thinking in relation to your particular positionality and, well, *you've* never existed before.'

I looked away from the poor imitations and up the mountain.

'And that's not to say that you don't see repetitive work or the same ideas coming back. Take all of these mattresses on my body for example. Tracey Emin really did a number on student taste. That's fine because sometimes artists have to look at the knowledge that other artists produce in order to start figuring out what they're going to make for themselves. You probably wished you were Maria Lassnig incarnate. You wanted her vision for yourself. But she was better at being Maria Lassnig than you were. If you don't mind me saying, you weren't very good at it. But you were only starting out, a tiny First Year away from home – you weren't very good at being yourself either, never mind someone else. In that gentle, raw, open moment, it was easier to try being her instead.'

(When do I get *good* at being myself . . . ?)

'Embarrassment is an important quality in that instance, because you intuited that you needed to move on. That's what art school teaching does quite well. It offers you all these fantastical ways to help you find *yourself* – and not in the cheesy *Eat Pray Love* sense. I mean, you're tasked with creating yourself, or versions of yourself. Of course, I don't believe there is an essentialist self; you can't peel back the layers and discover the true me – there's no human body at the heart of this rubbish heap. But there are selves being made over and over. Changing, changing all the time. That is learning. That is the generation of new knowledge. That is the entire point. Art school equips you so that you can go on your way, finding the versions of your practice that are the right ones for you, whoever you are right now, for whichever one of you is asking. Throw them on the pile!'

I threw my Maria Lassnig tributes like frisbees into his sides and Mark absorbed them like a giant shredder. I felt like I was in therapy or that this was the end of a hypnotism and Mark was helping me come to. *You've been in an accident. This is what happened. This is where you were hurt, and this is what we have done to save you.* I didn't know what to say.

'Don't worry. I don't expect my students to be perfectly articulate. Perhaps it is self-selecting, and not surprising, that often within the arts we come across people who find verbal communication difficult. If language has been difficult for us, maybe we've moved to another form of creativity. I, for one, read far more in the art that you make than in the words that you say, whether that's in the contents of those bin bags or whatever you're going to put in the degree show next week. In fact, I believe that art begins where language ends.'

I nodded. My essays had been marked down for not being sufficiently *historically authoritative*. It's like, I had an inkling of the words I wanted to say, but they never sounded clever enough. I'd submitted my dissertation a few weeks ago. Six thousand words on the expanded feminist praxis of digital sculpture-making in virtual reality, and I already knew it was terrible. I'd used a dry, academic voice that I didn't have any faith in, and I'd spent the autumn term banging my head against the library tables wishing I could submit a sculpture instead.

'Isn't it funny that often it is language that makes us anxious in art. It's when we have to write about it that we go all, *oh my God*, and glaze over as we do when somebody starts telling us the rules of a card game. Once we disentangle language from art and see language as a parallel, rather than something that pins art down or locks it up, then it becomes much easier to talk *in relation to* art, rather than *at* it; rather than have it be a head-on confrontation. Art doesn't operate in the same way language does. Art opens up new perspectives, new spaces, new ways of seeing. It allows us to say things we cannot say through any other means.'

I asked him why, if he was in charge of the course, he couldn't click his fingers – or whatever his equivalent was – and change the rules so that we didn't have to bother writing essays. When the tutors had finished marking my submission, could they 'forget' to email me my results? It's not like I *needed* to know.

'Child, if only that were the case. If only this were a true art school and not an art university.[17] If only I were a pile of art with my own free will and not a body melded to the floor of a building whose fate is decided by the state, a sprawling mechanism in and of itself that has no interest in art for art's sake. When I went to art school, it was free and very democratic. Now, we live in a world increasingly obsessed with metrics. It has this political feeling, right? You feel it?'

I nodded. The tutors had been going round the studios in the run-up to the degree show asking us to rate the school on the annual National Student Survey, the results of which were factored into league tables and graduate employment rankings.

'I hate it. It's an intrusion on our house. It would be brilliant if art didn't have to keep justifying its existence. It's a terrible backdrop for art-making – this expectation that artists need to prove their worth. Art is typically not good at doing that. It struggles with being measured, *and* with being measurable. That's because art says that there can't only be one form of knowledge construction; art is a slippery thing that creates knowledge in the gaps between these other fields. It defies metrics altogether. As I said, as much as we might try to wrangle it, art

17. Kerri Jefferis made this distinction in the video essay 'So Free, So Powerless, So Psychopath', 2016.

defies language too. I *wish* we didn't have to grade you. It's a farce. Art isn't shackled to the confines of truth or numbers. It's not bound by strict methodologies. That's *why* we love it. But it can be hard to keep that love when art is being made – and then examined – by an institution like ours. It's a good job nobody ever asks what grade you got on an art degree when you leave. Ha! Now, show me what else you have brought before you demoralize me any further. I cannot allow myself to think about the state of the world for too long.'

Right. The bags. What else did I have in the bags? I got a second-year piece out next, this huge roll of paper. I'd used it one night when we had an open studio,[18] and I'd left instructions that somebody always had to be holding the pen. Participants could do whatever they wanted with the pen, but they couldn't move on until they'd got someone else to agree to take the baton. By the end of the night, the paper resembled the inside of a toilet cubicle in a shoddy bar. I hated it like I've always hated those toilets, hovering over a broken seat and wondering why drunk people always have Sharpies on them. Don't get me wrong, it was sweet watching people on the night, and it was funny watching them negotiate their way out of the position. But the process was far more interesting than the outcome.

18. Open studios are events where studio groups invite the public to see works in progress and live performances.

I hadn't unrolled the paper since that night. Doing so now in front of Mark made me realize how much my work had changed between first and second year; I'd stopped being so precious and started having fun with it. If I'd had stabilizers on, I never noticed them come off.

'Maybe it happened when you realized that the school was there to catch you? At its best, art education is like scaffolding. It's a container within which you can fill the content bespoke to your needs and interests. We try to create an environment that allows you to take owner-ship of your own learning, but we're still there in the background – because that moment before you learn to ride the bike on your own needs to be supported. That's why we have the lectures, the seminars, the projects. The visiting artists who tell you how they ride their own bikes. It's a trust fall but we want you to be covered from all angles, so other students are there to catch you too. You can see that here in the work you made. You weren't thinking about aesthetics. You wanted to see what would happen if you opened your art up to others. It might look naff, but it's quite sentimental really, and I like it because you were using one of the most import-ant things we gave you.'

'What?'

'Your peers. For the past few years, you've been in a studio with five or six regulars in your corner of the room. You've all been making work, putting it on the wall. You've noticed what the others are doing. They've followed the progression of your thinking. You've exchanged comments, you've had lunch together. You've complained about something someone said – maybe you've complained about the faculty, how awful I am. You've brought recommendations to each other for that Kara Walker exhibition at Camden Art Centre, and you've done a field trip to Jumana Manna's show at the Chisenhale. You've lent each other Chris Kraus books, not knowing if they were novels or something between fiction and non-fiction. And after eating dinner around a laptop screen, where you have been watching James Baldwin speeches on YouTube, you've got the bus home together, and spoken about your families. It was all learning, every second of it. The studio provides a space in which to enact those *other* modes of teaching in the form of peer-to-peer conversation. I *know* you hate this gratuitous scribble on your beloved roll of paper, but it is evidence of so much.'

I'd never thought about my friends as forming a part of my education.

'I hope that art is moving away from the me-me-me of individual practice to the we of making culture together. Knowledge isn't held by one person and transferred to another. Knowledge is gained through an exchange – through actually practising something. Most of us have imposter syndrome. You pretend you know what you're doing until you're way down the line and suddenly think, oh, I know what I'm doing now. It's only because

I've pretended a few times, that I've got to this point. Well, peer-to-peer can really open up space to roleplay being an artist in a network of other artists. You shouldn't underestimate what that means. Think about what you've gained from being here. You are about to graduate with a peer group of around two hundred people who are interested in the arts, enthusiastic, aiming for all sorts of specialisms – people who might provide you with opportunities later on, encourage-ment, or a couch to sleep on; and if an opportunity pops up in Birmingham or Shanghai, you'll be so thankful for that couch. There isn't much in the way of support for artists, but a network is certainly one of them. We need to take that seriously, and not think of it as a by-product of being on an art course, but as a central tenet of art education – community-building as a fundamental part of learning, and a fundamental part of your adult life to come. Because, if you understand your peers and where they're headed, where their concerns are, you're better placed to move with them into the future.'

I really thought my small friendship group would meet post-graduate life as a unified force. But what I didn't know was how many people were planning on leaving London because they couldn't afford to stay *or* they simply didn't want the shitty work–life balance that stubborn idiots like me were willing to put up with. It didn't take long before the majority left the group chat, got other jobs. Mark's description of a successful art school was dependent on a strong social network, but I couldn't come in half as much as I wanted to because I had to work to afford to be there. I wasn't the only one. Other students had caring responsibilities, illnesses; or they were shy, they hadn't clicked with anybody, or they had to commute hours to get there and back.

'It's worth adding that in listening to each other, you're actively deconstructing the idea that I'm a figure of singular authority.'

We had moaned a fair amount about the tutors, he was right about that.

'Listening to your peers is painless compared to the student–tutor relationship. The best way to get the most out of art school is to be alert to guru teaching. There's a temptation for the student – how do I put this without it sounding wrong . . . Sometimes the student wants to fall in love with the teacher.'

Er . . .

'In terms of the dynamic. The student wants to believe in the teacher but the teacher has to keep reminding the student that they shouldn't do that. That's the wrong approach. They, as the teacher, are fallible. They are not the one almighty holder of knowledge. Guru teaching is when students follow teachers unquestioningly. I have to be vigilant because you don't want the tutor who, in a crit, would say, *you know what would make this piece really work, the thing that I do in my own art practice.*

That cannot happen. Daddy does not know best. I don't want to be Daddy!'

I'd had run-ins with tutors who weren't attuned to this, and the things they'd said were burnt in my memory to this day. For example, there was the one tutorial when a posh, very conceptual painter had turned his nose up at the latest still life I'd painted (during my Maria Lassnig phase), and asked if I only painted because I thought I could make money from it. Now, I couldn't tell if his tone was meant to imply the rest of a sentence that went '. . . because there's no way someone will buy this' or '. . . because here in the hallowed art school halls, we don't make art to *sell* it. That's *sacrilege*.' God, I wish I'd had the nerve to ignore him, or better yet, challenge him. My halls had a window gallery on the side of the building, what with it being full of art students, and a man knocked on the door to buy the still life for his mum's birthday. I sold it to him for £100 and I couldn't believe my luck. I pictured a whole new life for myself where I got to do the thing I loved for a living. I tried to tell my tutor about my good fortune, and he looked disgusted. I couldn't under-stand how making money directly from my art could ever be a bad thing; and while I didn't want to fall in love with my tutor, or have him fall in love with me, I *did* want his approval, and that's close enough.

'Don't take any of this as gospel. What did I say about words and art and truth? Don't listen to me! Especially don't listen to someone who is made up of all the art nobody wants. I don't have the answers. You think I do because I've become this encrusted, institutionalized bodiless voice that speaks from up high on his mountain. I'm an old man. Your job is to ignore the image of power. Climb all over it. Disrespect it, disrespect me. I can take it. I will take your paper too. Give it its grace before it's gone for ever, lost somewhere in my churning mess.'

I am so bad at ignoring the image of power, but I mean, we all are. We are programmed to be subservient. I listened to Mark, and I pelted my artwork into his crust like a javelin. But as soon as it got sucked into his mass, I resumed my role as a good student who played by the rules.

'Is there anything else in there? Any fresh wounds in the form of third-year disasters?'

We were almost at the end. I looked at the bottom of the bin bag and found the first sculptures I'd made after I'd been exiled from the world of painting for being a money-grabbing scoundrel. The sculptures were plaster casts of various fruits. When they came out looking exactly like the fruit I'd cast them from, I wasn't satisfied like I thought I'd be. So, I let a row of lemons rot along my windowsill until the yellow turned from white to green and blue and black. I took them back into the studio when they were shrivelled and ugly, carrying them wrapped in kitchen roll in my hands. The plaster shells and dried lemons were knocking together at the bottom of the bag and they were so small I wasn't sure

Mark would be able to see them from all the way up there.

By final year, I'd learnt that contemporary art was whatever you wanted it to be. Whatever you could get away with. The more tenuous the claim, the more avant-garde it was. Pushing the boat out meant pushing up against the limits of the field – innovating – and I'd seen students do all sorts. Someone built a human-sized cat tower. Someone else delivered a video essay using a Craig David deepfake. A student in the year above announced they were losing their virginity in a live event that people could buy tickets to, only to hoodwink the audience into watching a sexless dance. Then, at the Christmas party, where Mark had pulled an aux cable and a disco ball out from somewhere inside him, I remember one artwork that turned into an emergency. A girl cast her body in massive blocks of plaster. The plan was that other students would excavate her over the course of the night, like she was a fossil, or a crystal, or a Kinder surprise. We all learnt plaster was exothermic that day when the girl inside was sort of being cooked. Festivities were put on hold and the excavation ramped up, while Mark quite rightly told her off. (The danger *did* make it a lot more memorable, though; got to give her that.)

I picked up my straightforward plaster artworks of dying lemons and held them up. I told Mark they weren't disasters, they just weren't very interesting given the madness everybody else was coming up with. I didn't throw these pieces at the mountain. I placed them gently around the edges, watching the tideline of bigger objects grind the plaster to dust.

I plucked one of the lemons that hadn't been absorbed yet. I said that this is how I had been feeling lately, like food as it approaches its expiry date. I didn't think I was a very exceptional artist. I didn't think I had come into my own yet. I was on the cusp of leaving school for good, and I was already on the turn. I wanted a do-over now that I knew what was what. I could find myself sooner. I could find my friends straight away. I could fight the tutors now that I knew I had permission to fight them.

'This isn't really the end. I haven't done my job if you think you're about to vanish into thin air. You're not going anywhere except out of the building. Remember what I said before – art school has given you the tools and the know-how to be able to interrogate your practice and yourself *for ever*. When these three years come to an end, you don't stop knowing that; you don't stop having ideas. In fact, you might have more ideas because you will have lived more.'

I was not convinced, and Mark could see it on my face.

'This whole thing is not a forward trajectory, and I don't say that to worry you. I say it in the hope that you can give yourself a break. Look at the work you have made. You haven't dealt with art in a vertical sense, constantly building on the last piece, and making sure the next thing is better and bigger and more critically sound than the last. No one does that. It's not possible, and it's not interesting either. We're not robots! Artists move along a bumpy horizontal axis. They experiment, and they go on tangents. They roll on the floor and pick up debris. They enjoy the adventure, or life gets in the way, and they stop, and they return. Isn't that freeing? Put all of this on hold whenever you want to, and come back to art when you need to. There really is no rush, child. Stop thinking about time and endings. Stop thinking about expired lemons. The best is yet to come.'

I put the lemon on the mountain. It helped that as we'd been talking, I could see all the students who had come before me in the kaleidoscope of art he was made of. The awkward drawings, smashed glass. Fabric torn, and canvases obliterated in the woodchipper of his body. People who are known for making very good art have probably made loads of bad stuff we've never seen. I wanted to climb into the pile so that I had no choice but to stay – but when I picked up the empty bin bags, something clinked.

'*I heard that*. You have something else to scrap.'

Oh yeah. I'd forgotten. I put my arm in and pulled them out. It was a thank-you card and a bottle of wine. Mum had called to remind me.

'That's very kind.'

I tossed them at the mountain and said my nervous goodbyes.

Royal
Tunbridge Wills

I used to know a horrible boy called William who wore a suit around university, complete with cravat. Always the loudest in the room, we got into a fight at a party once because he said he hated people from Liverpool. He told me he was from Royal Tunbridge Wells, and his house didn't have a number, it had a name. Allegedly I 'went' for him. I tried to bite him? I didn't realize I was willing to die for the scouse republic.

A few years had passed since graduation and I hadn't heard anything about Royal Tunbridge Wills until I got an email inviting me to his debut solo exhibition. In an ideal world, I would have ignored it. But I had realized it was all well and good thinking of myself as an artist under the privacy of my own floorboards, but the art world existed outside of my mental breakdown and so I made a pact with myself to start going to stuff. I would go to openings and stand on the edges of the room, looking at the relaxed backs of strangers in the way of the art. I'd swipe white wine, fail to speak to anybody, and hope my presence would count for something, even though I

would have preferred red wine or a can of Coke.
A calimocho,[19] a career.

Royal Tunbridge Wills was exhibiting in one of those
Mayfair white cubes with glass showroom walls.
The kind of gallery that has a new-car smell, where the
woman at the desk looks openly disappointed when
someone like me wanders in because I'm obviously
not there to shop.

The opening was packed. I hated that it was packed. It
was hot and bright and the pavements had not a chewy
in sight. Nothing for that artist Ben Wilson to paint on,
the one that paints miniature scenes on all the chewing
gum that decorates the streets of London. I braced
myself to go into the gallery alone. The friends who had
managed to stay in the city had been acting weird lately.
Scheduling hang-outs in shared calendars with beginning and end times as though our relationships were
now strictly business. Everyone was so overworked that
when we did manage to *squeeze each other in*, I'd get a
'thank you for coming' in place of 'hello'; and if I did see
someone at an opening, they would eventually cut me
off mid-sentence because we had *already spoken for
five minutes and we really should do our best to speak
to other people now*. As in, they wanted to work the
room. Who gives a shit about the room! Should I give a

---

19. If a mix of red wine and Coke is good enough for Spanish
teenagers, then it's good enough for me.

shit about the room? But then, I half-understood where it was coming from – it was for the same reason I'd made this stupid pact with myself.

Wills was showing the same art he put in the degree show, way back when. It was shit then and it looked even worse now. He used to buy these big, fuck-off canvases and deface them with either a bland pattern or a single bucket-filled shape. I'd have to bite my tongue watching him apply acrylic on top of oil paint, and later roll my eyes when I heard him complaining about the quality of the paint he was using, because the top layer would awkwardly peel off. In group crits, he would change his tune completely. See, he *knew* it was fat over lean,[20] and actually, this piece was an attempt to contradict traditional methods. A real maverick. Even the paint cringed. I don't really like saying anybody's art is shit, because I think when people use words like 'good' or 'bad' as if they are objective truths, they're usually confusing quality with taste. But I was standing in the showroom in front of those same pieces, which had been salvaged with varnish to give them a slick, buyable finish and hold the remaining paint in place, and they looked dire.

The press release told a different story. It introduced Wills as 'a leading figure in the contemporary,

20. If layers of oil paint do not contain as much oil content as each other, the ones with less oil can draw it from the richer layers, causing the paint to crack.

transatlantic practice of Zombie Formalism, in which antiquated values of materiality, originality and process come head to head *to head* in a raucous challenge on the surface of the canvas.' People could say literally whatever, and as long as it was packaged in the right way, it had authority. But Wills made art that didn't ask questions. He excelled in a particular style of painterly abstraction that's just there, and there's a lot of it. There's nothing more conservative than that look. It conveys nothing, and the fact that so many rich people spend money on it leads me to believe they're dead inside. Must be how it got the name.[21]

I dropped the exhibition handout on the floor of the busy room and let everybody walk all over it. Lonely, sweaty. The staff from the gallery kept slipping between visitors and making conversation, and it seemed to annoy Wills, who was batting them away. It was so hot that the person next to me said they felt feverish. Wills was in the middle of the room, occasionally patting his face with a silk pocket square, and I was close enough that I overheard him berating his 'old pals' from university; the same clique who insisted on taking the stairs to the third-floor studios, rather than the lift, because they wanted to keep fitting into an Acne Studios medium-slim fit. *Fuck off.*

21. No, but, for real, Zombie Formalism was coined by Walter Robinson in his article 'Flipping and the Rise of Zombie Formalism', Artspace, 2014.

'Where have you all been? It's like you dropped off the face of the Earth. *Tell me* you haven't been sitting on your hands waiting for something like this to happen.'

He spread his arms wide, hitting multiple guests in the process.

'I've always believed it's the most toxic mythology, this belief that artists have to wait for somebody to come knocking.'

He took a big swig of wine and gave the empty glass to someone who didn't even work there.

'You must destroy that notion. Destroy the idea that a capricious patron is waiting around the corner to drop cash in your lap. They're not like that. Trust me. Hope keeps us shackled. In chains. Handcuffs! Naughty. No, no, you have to ask for what you want. Go out and get it. Pull yourself up by the bootstraps like I've done.'

Without turning, he took a drink from someone who was not a waiter.

'And it's not always fun, but it is *work* after all. For instance, it took me months to find an art student who would run my social media *for the experience.*[22] And this girl, she won't let me post pictures. Everything *has* to be

22. Art world code meaning working for free.

a video. That's the next generation talking. She says there's two ways for me to go about it. I either have to make my audience love me or they *really* need to hate me.'

I couldn't imagine anyone even liking this man.

'But how could anyone hate me? No, I want love, of course. My intern said that I can engineer love by creating desire or relatability. It's like advertising – you show people something they don't have, and in doing so, you create in them a desire they didn't have before. That way, they'll buy whatever you're selling to quench their new thirst. To become you. Who wouldn't want *this*? We tried that route first. I would show my studio because it's so big everyone wanted it. Even people who've never made art before. But more than that, I would let people into my lifestyle. Holidays, parties – the art in my friends' homes made for great content in that respect.'

My friends didn't have art in their homes. They had outstanding bills and silverfish.

'That was fine for a while, but I had to do the filming, and I had an intern for that. So, we worked smarter, not harder. She introduced me to *satisfying videos.* Those silly little clips that people watch on a loop because they have nothing going on inside their head . . .'

Or we *want* to have nothing inside our heads, if only for a moment.

'She has me doing various action paintings on scraps I have lying around. But I tell you what, she was right. We have everything rigged up, so I only need to pour paint on to the centre of a canvas – and it only has to be a small thing – because the canvas is attached to a drill, and when I pull the trigger –'

I watched him pretend to fire a gun.

 – 'the paint spins out, and when I stop –' he blew the imaginary smoke away – 'it's a psychedelic blur.'

He was desecrating *Art Attack*.

'I also fill balloons with paint and throw darts at them. Or we zoom in on dripping paint. If I play a popular song over the top, fans of the music stick around to listen. Or I squeegee it! One of *those* videos is coming up to a million views – Gerhard Richter needs to take a leaf out of my book, because I don't actually have to finish a single painting. It's genius. As the girl explains, artists who post finished paintings on social media come off like they're bragging. The audience resents the person with all the time in the world to paint. Work-in-progress clips, even if they're progressing to nowhere, are much more relatable. Because we're all a work in progress. Aren't we, boys and girls?'

His audience dutifully nodded.

'The plan is to hit a healthy follower count, and then I can get signed with a talent agency who can book me for branded partnerships, talks, that sort of thing, and that's only one of my interns. I found another to take care of web design, a third to write my artist statement. I like that one. He really found my place in the canon – did you read the press release?'

A person fainted on the other side of the room. Wills carried on spouting bullshit, even though he was sweating so much I thought he might conk out next.

'That's the only way to go about it, and, as I said, it works. Take this show for example – they *wanted* me. They *begged* me to exhibit. *Constant* emails asking for my availability, absolutely dying for a call.'

A second person fainted. I couldn't wait around any longer. Like, yes, I was waiting around in general. He was right about that. Waiting for the stars to align, for Sadie Coles to hit me up[23] or for a tame sculpture I posted on Instagram to go viral for no reason so that I could have fame and fortune and not have to drag myself to agonizing nights like this. I wasn't sitting on my hands. I was here, wasn't I? Not for long.

When I got to the exit, a woman jumped in front of me. She had a lanyard round her neck, and she was wearing the rushed make-up I recognized on Londoners who only had time for mascara through a compact mirror on the tube. Our faces were close. She asked if

23. Sadie Coles is an English art dealer who runs an art gallery named after herself.

I was an artist, and I think my heart actually skipped a beat.

'We have a gap in the calendar if you are looking to exhibit.'

Oh my God, it was happening.

'We offer three metres of wall space for £660.'

Oh my God, she was going to pay me.

'Six metres for £1,320, nine for £1,980.'

Oh my God, if I showed everything I'd made recently, I could fill the full nine metres. Stars aligning. Lottery numbers. I was an artist.

'The package includes installation and set-up. It's all in the leaflet.'

The package? The leaflet? I looked down to see one in my hands.

'Yeah, the package also covers a late-night opening reception like tonight. We'll list the show on our website, take care of invigilation, and we're able to give you pricing advice and sales support. We do take commission. That's standard. But we also print invitation cards so you can pass them out to family and friends. Are you local? I can't tell where your accent's from. But don't worry if not, because we currently have thirty thousand on our mailing list and a few people from that always pop along, so it's a fantastic way to expand your audience. Plus, if you show with us, and then success-fully refer a friend to exhibit too, we'll put you in the annual raffle so that you have another chance at getting an exhibition.'

She looked me up and down.

'We have another space on Brick Lane if that's more your style?'[24]

It was the heat, or the drink, or our mis-matched energy – I don't know – but it took me a second to register that Wills had paid for his exhibition. Or his parents had. His trust fund. The gallery wasn't paying him. He was paying the gallery. The gallery wasn't begging him to exhibit because they adored his art and his ugly spin videos. They wanted the money and he obliged. A four-figure obligation. I smiled at the woman and put the leaflet in my pocket, as if I had any interest in her scheme. (I couldn't afford to be interested! To be honest, that's what pissed me off.)

Was he cheating? Was that unfair for me to say, or more unfair of him to do? I couldn't quite decide. If he was so intent on living this 100-emoji go-getter lifestyle, why didn't he admit he'd got the show because he was rich enough to enjoy free will? The lie undid him. He wanted the external validation of a real curator from a real

24. We pulled these prices for these exact wall space measurements from Brick Lane Gallery's website in 2022.

gallery to think his work was important enough to show to other people. This show was simply Wills keeping up appearances. He was a megalomaniac. He wanted to carry on being the loudest in the room – the person who could buy the biggest canvases, bewitch the most desperate interns.

I turned back. I had the sudden urge to confront him, but in that same second, the entire room changed. Half the crowd fell to the floor and the other half were legging it. Everyone was screaming bloody murder because, in the centre of the mess, Royal Tunbridge Wills was covered in lanyard-wearing gallery staff who were ripping off his skin. I thought I must have been having another one of my episodes because I swear I could see blood turning to steam in the summer heat and dyeing the showroom's white walls bright red. It was spurting out of him like a fountain, and I watched the gallery's interns clamber over each other to keep Wills' blood from reaching the walls lest they ruin the goods they were still clearly hoping to sell.

The woman who'd tried to flog me nine metres of temporary wall space looked at me after she was done gnawing on Wills' left foot. She pointed. The other staff followed her finger. They stood. Started walking. I thought it wasn't quite a cult, more like multi-level marketing. Invest in yourself, invest in your network, invest in your future. I'd seen this before, when my aunties did a stint with Avon. It had nothing to do with the quality of the liquid eyeliner on offer and everything to do with recruiting more people to sell it. I'm good, thanks.

And that's when I remembered to run.

I didn't know where the fuck I was going, but my legs did. They took me to the institutional art world. I ran through the Royal Academy's courtyard and banged my fists against the big front door. Someone on the other side cracked the letterbox an inch and told me the building closed at 6 p.m, OK? *But if you don't let me in, I'm going to die.* Burlington House was a seventeenth-century fortress – a sanctuary for the learned societies. It would never be breached. I explained that I was an artist – one of *them* – and the voice asked me if I had been elected by ballot to become a Royal Academician. *A magician?* It asked me who my parents were. I didn't know what to say. The letterbox snapped shut. *No provenance*, I heard it moan slowly, as if we both had all the time in the world. *Move on.*

I tried the commercial art world after that, ending up at the translucent doors of Pace Gallery[25] where I could make out the silhouette of a slinky figure. I pulled on the door handle but they pulled back from the other side. I caught my breath and explained what was happening,

---

25. Pace Gallery was established in Boston in 1960 and currently has three spaces in the US, with further galleries in London, Hong Kong, Seoul, Tokyo and Geneva.

and apologized for my intrusion. They were quiet for a moment and then they asked me how many buyers I knew. Quickly, they challenged me, name your closest contacts, as well as any works they have purchased in the past twelve months. But I didn't know any buyers. I only knew artists, such as myself. I was an artist and I wanted to come in. They told me that while they were very sorry to hear about my situation, exposure to zombies made me less valuable to the market. I promised they hadn't got to me yet – if only they'd let me in, they could look all over my body for bite marks and find nothing. The silhouette faded. I spat at the glass and pushed on.

What was even left? The independent art world? Harder to find. It wasn't a whole world, more like an archipelago. I headed east, not stopping until I heard the mixed reactions of an open-mic night. It was dark now, and I was scared the zombies were going to jump out from behind me at any second. I walked in. The stage was being shared by comedians, musicians, poets, a spoken-word artist and a mime. I sobbed into the mic and the entire room stopped what they were doing to discuss. I watched them take a vote, one eye on the door waiting for an attack to hit. The group decided they could, indeed, save me – oh, thank God – but they couldn't put me up for long because they didn't have any money. They told me I could leaflet the open mic for them in exchange for a couch to sleep on and a bowl of lentil soup. I started crying because I don't like lentil soup and I had a newfound hatred for leaflets. All I could think about was how much I wanted to live an artistic life and how little it wanted anything to do with me.

Once upon a time, I did all-nighters to play with paint. I grew up and realized that there was no career ladder for me to climb so that I could carry on being an artist. But, not to worry because there were always people offering to show me the way. I just had to give them all of my gold coins and everything would be OK. I could spend coins to have my own exhibition, I could spend coins to sponsor my Instagram posts so that more people would see my work. I could spend coins on a cold studio space that might make me feel closer to my goals. We could *all* pay to enter an art prize, the reward of which would be a cut of the many gold coins we supplied. If I didn't like the sound of that, there were always masterclasses to pay for, or I could spend my very limited earnings on joining exclusive newsletters that shared opportunities to subscribers who were so hungry to compete for the right to be an artist that they were willing to spend all of these coins upfront. If only I spent enough coins, I could climb my way up the ladder. I could be an artist. I could pay to win.

Once upon a time, I believed the ladder was real. But the ladder was simply an image of a way out created by zombies who knew they could capitalize on our all-nighter joy. They understood full well the conditions did not allow poor artists to thrive, and they knew we had nowhere to run.

We thought they were going to help us, but they only helped themselves.

And now Royal Tunbridge Wills was dead.

Cilla Black

During the last term of university, there was a lecture down on the calendar as 'Professional Development'. The tutor had asked the audience who was excited about graduation, and because I was the only one that didn't put my hand up, she obviously chose me as the contestant. The lecture hall was always transforming like a stage, and tonight there was a pink-and-blue LCD backdrop, three chairs in a row, a divider, and a fourth stool alone on the other side. That's where I ended up sitting waiting for *Blind Date* to start – you know that TV show from years ago? I thought Cilla Black was dead.

'Welcome to another *Blind Date*! Let's meet three eye-catching professionals all hoping to catch our picker's eyes tonight. Bring in the pros!'

Everyone started clapping and I heard shuffling from behind the screen as my suitors took their place.

'They love ya, they love ya, they do. Don't they look smart?'

Maybe it was a good thing I'd been singled out. Final year had triggered stress psoriasis and the doctor had been no use. Of course they hadn't. I needed my life to change, not my body. I needed a guaranteed income on graduating, not topical steroid creams.

'Hello, number one, what's ya name and where d'ya come from?'

'I'm Gregory, and I'm from Kensington.'

I grew up in Liverpool's Kensington, the polar opposite of London's.

'Greg, what d'ya do, chuck?'

'I'm an accountant to the world's finest artists, and if you pick me tonight, I promise you can always count on me.'

Jesus fucking Christ.

'Hello, number two, what's ya name and where d'ya come from?'

'I'm Nikita, and I'm from Manchester.'

Better?

'What d'ya do, our Nik?'

'I'm a Museum Education Coordinator, and if I get picked tonight, I'll teach you *everything* you need to know.'

Everyone oohed, and I felt bad because I couldn't give two shits about Museum Education Coordination.

'Finally, number three, what's ya name and where d'ya come from?'

'I'm Eleanor and I'm from Edinburgh.'

'What d'ya do, Ellie from Edinburgh?'

'I'm the head of Public Relations at a boutique arts agency, and if you choose me, I'll take *very good* care of our *relationship*.'

Did Professional Development mean showing us the arts jobs that weren't 'artist'?

'Enjoy *Blind Date*, you're all gorgeous. I'll see you pros in a mo.'

The music was so loud nobody could hear the continuous groan coming from deep inside me. I had friends who had gone for peripheral work that only existed because of artists but didn't actually involve making any art. I knew there were front-of-house positions available in museums, but the same friends had warned me off them. Tickets and information meant hanging out with other staff who wished they were full-time artists instead, and fielding requests from visitors who wished for exactly the same. Some of them would bring in portfolios to show the museum's curators, but to no avail; it might have been the done thing once upon a time, but nowadays, haughty curators looked down on the artists brave enough to put themselves forward. So, my friends looked down on the curators and gave out the email addresses of senior staff to anyone who wanted them. Yeah, I would get fired for that as well.

What these museums failed to mention on the job description was that front of house is also a stand-in for social services. There were very lonely visitors who didn't come to the museum for the art but because it was the only place they could go. They came every day because it was public, free, warm in the winter, cool in the summer; there were bathrooms with toilets, sinks, and much-needed privacy; and there was some dignity provided just by being in the building. It was difficult for minimum-wage staff to provide the care and attention and time to these visitors, but it was up to them to try; the curators were busy hiding in their offices.

'They certainly are an attractive trio. Very influential. Let's meet the art student who has to choose one of them as her mentor. Her name's Quest and she's from Liverpool – ay, like me, girl!'

Cilla Black asked what I wanted to be when I grew up. I told her I wanted to be an artist, and she patted my arm.

'Well, Cilla's looking after ya, sweetheart. All three of our pros are fab, but have you got a fab question for them? Fire away, chuck.'

I wanted to know if she was happy presenting TV shows and occasionally starring in pantomimes. I knew my Liverpool history – I knew she'd started out as a singer and that Brian Epstein had collected her around the same time he got hold of The Beatles. But then The Beatles went off to America and he told a young Cilla she should do telly instead. Sure, Cilla Black was a household name but TV wasn't her first love. Why had she patted my arm when I'd said I wanted to be an artist? Does no one think I can do it?

But I didn't say that. My actual question was formatted in the symmetrical, poetic way this show communicated in:

'Being an artist is my dream. What makes *you* think you can wake me up?'

'Oh, she's feisty. Number one, what's yer answer?'

I listened to the posh voice on the other side of the screen.

'Having done the accounts for hundreds of artists over the years, I know that money is *everything*. I've been there for the peaks and valleys of many a career, and I know there isn't much logic to success. There are artists worth millions overnight, seemingly at random. One dealer values a work highly and that's that. We all do. Taste aligns for a moment and, pop, Flora Yukhnovich is on top and we like Rococo now.

'You might have heard stories of Picasso scribbling on a napkin to pay for a meal because even his worst effort was meant to be worth something. But you might not be too familiar with the other end of the spectrum – the sad tales of artists who had to bet on themselves because nobody else would. The artists who take out loans to put on their own shows. Artists like Frederick J. Brown, whose talent might have deserved the same level of financial success but it never happened, and so he felt the need to take out loans he couldn't afford, bet on himself, and ultimately he ended up bankrupt. Other artists have no choice but to max out credit cards when galleries don't pay them quickly enough. It's rough.

'Don't get me wrong, I am a huge fan of the arts, and I respect everybody in this room for studying such a fine subject. But respect is not guaranteed outside of these walls. You don't want to be disrespected your whole life, do you? Gosh, I see wannabe actors leading ghost tours around Soho. I see wannabe musicians busking on the streets for pennies. I see wannabe artists working in cafés where they might get to design a nice chalkboard to frame the entrées. I feel sorry for these people. I respect the arts but if my children ever wanted to make a go of it, I would let them go to art school, but then I would say, *come on, you've had your fun. Come with me into the office so that I can teach you how to do a job that other people can't embarrass you for.*

'And there's lots to do in the office. Lots for artists to keep track of, which means lots for us to double- and triple-check. Of course, plenty of self-employed artists do their own bookkeeping.'

There was a pause.

'You're all looking at me like you didn't know that was required of you. It's quite simple. If you add up how much it costs you to do your work, you can subtract your expenditure from your total income and only pay taxes on the remaining sum. I'll give you that for free – because maybe if you do your books right, you can earn enough to pay me to do them for you. There are plenty of items you should be expensing. Materials, tools, software, travel, studio rent and even tickets to galleries, which you can always put down as research. Canvases can jump into the thousands when you get big enough. If you're a performance artist, even better. Expense everything! Expense your clothes, your make-up, your toothpaste. You need all of those things to perform, don't you? Expense your domestic bills according to the percentage of time you are in character in your own home. Take Lorraine Kelly as a precedent.[26] But gosh, doesn't that sound . . . *desperate*? Clutching at withered receipts in an attempt to shield yourself from the tax-man. If you choose me, I promise you it'll be a *tax relief*.'

I half-expected the room to boo him, but everyone looked like they were questioning what they were still doing in art school.

'Number two, what does the museum have to say about Quest's dream to become an artist?'

---

26. Lorraine Kelly is a TV presenter who once got taken to court by the Scottish government over her taxes, where the judge ruled she qualified for tax breaks because she wasn't appearing as herself on TV, but actually as a persona of herself.

'Oh, well, I think artists are the most wonderful people. But there's an inherent, humiliating truth in that I can't think about being an artist without thinking of making something that is worth bankrolling, and it never happened for me. There are so many wonderful jobs that support art – organizations need technicians, producers, art handlers, archivists, human resources, fundraisers, accountants, bid writers, cleaners, researchers, marketers, cooks, graphic designers, security, merchandisers, buyers, photographers and a few trustees sprinkled on top. Outside of museums, there are printers, framers, art material manufacturers, studio managers, auctions, art law firms, and then there is education, which is where I landed. I thought I could make a job out of art-making, but as it turns out, what you can make a job out of is teaching other people to try.

'With my artist hat on, the most contact I ever got from museums were invitations to run quick workshops. I was on a few panel talks. Another place asked me to introduce an artist's screening. It is an awkward thing to intuit but I always felt that these galleries put me on their secondary, public programming, rather than their main exhibition programme, as a way to tick boxes without having me interfere too much with the healthier budget over in the exhibition department. They would throw a hundred pounds at their own lack of diversity, and as the accountant to my right can attest, a few hundred-pound lump sums a year are not going to pay anyone's bills. I felt quite embarrassed that I kept allowing them to use me like that, when, really, I wasn't getting much in return. It was almost like these museums wanted under-represented artists to stay under-represented.'

Cilla, who was standing in line with the divider, looked over to me and then back at number two.

'That's all I have to say, really. I'd done enough work-shops that I had a good CV to apply for an education role at a museum, and now I have all the benefits of a salary. I try to have an impact where I can, like other art educators in universities, colleges and prisons. But when I speak to early-career artists, it almost feels inevitable that they'll come to the same conclusions. So no, I don't know anything about dreams. But if the nightmare gets too much, I'll be here to guide you through it.'

The room was heavy.

'Well, then, last but not least, number three. Can *you* make Quest's dreams come true?'

'That's not how I understood her question. I believe she was daring us to sell her a bigger dream than that of the artist, and while I don't know if there is one, I can certainly try.'

There were going to be Ofcom complaints about how depressing this episode of *Blind Date* was.

'So, I work in PR at a creative agency, and I specialize in comms. I have to say, I love my job. People say that art speaks for itself, but the truth is, a lot of audiences don't know what they're looking at, and they might not be able to get as far into the work as they'd like to without a bit of help. They might not even bother coming into the gallery if they aren't told what's inside. But advertising can help people overcome that threshold psychology, and so too can language. Many artists struggle to talk about their own work, and when curators get hold of it, they can struggle to interpret that work for the public. We assume we're all making sense to each other in a room like this, but go outside and you'll find that not everyone is versed in artspeak. Maybe more pressing is the fact that the government did a survey of adults in England back in 2011 which revealed one in seven of us have a reading age of between nine and eleven.

'I work with artists. We've got big names on the books, and a few have come to us via social media. We think about what an artist's unique selling point is, and we go for simple, punchy, memorable elevator pitches over the more convoluted artist statements you might be trained to write. They have their place, I agree. But if you don't learn how to talk about your work in a more efficient way, it might put people off. I sympathize with that. In the past, it would have been up to the critics, curators and art historians to describe your work for you. But I also think it's a good thing artists don't have to wait for other people. It's a service they can buy, and much more comes with it; we work with artists to determine a brand identity, maximize their discoverability, create strong content plans, a clear web presence, and even offer media training. Not everyone comes prepackaged with charisma, but we can help out.

'At the agency, we aim to bring in staff who really understand how creatives think. Book translators always work from their second language back into their mother tongue, and we're the same. We want artists working *for* us. We want artists helping us to support other artists. But at the end of the day, I know I'd rather be in a job that doesn't require so much support. Art sure needs a lot of it, but it does have transferable skills. I wonder if you'd like to transfer them my way?'

Cilla started walking to the front of the stage.

'Who is our picker gonna go for? Will it be the accountant, the educator or the agent? The decision is yours.'

The audience were shouting numbers while they thought I was deliberating over my future mentor. I wasn't. I was thinking about the illustrators I followed online who were living it large selling vinyl stickers, keyrings, fabric hangings and digital downloads, and who were making a healthy living as a result of having fans willing to pay for designs of original characters. Other artists were posting studio vlogs on YouTube and getting paid directly through the platform and by doing sponsorship deals. I would rather have gone to a lecture from those artists, because this was more like a consolation prize. I was also thinking about how, if I wanted to be an artist, I was going to have to be my own accountant, administrator, workshop facilitator, studio manager, technician, art handler, photographer, archivist and marketing team on top of everything else. Every step of the career I wanted seemed insurmountable, and it didn't help that the university seemed to be nudging me towards other ladders I might want to climb.

I heard a slurp. Cilla Black was licking an orange slice rubbed down with a crumbly brown OXO cube.[27] The soundtrack changed and she threw the used orange stage left. I told her I wanted to go with number one. He was clearly the richest so I thought he'd be the least offended when I never got in touch.

27. Cilla Black describes her fascination with eating orange slices rubbed with OXO cubes in an episode of *Eating with . . .* produced by the BBC, 2006.

Get a Job

In the winter of 1983, the artist David Hammons rolled out a rug next to other street vendors in the streets of New York and lined up his wares. He wasn't selling second-hand jackets and jewellery like his neighbours; Hammons was selling snowballs in all different sizes. He never publicized the event ahead of time. It was a scam, a laugh, an absurdist excuse to interact with people, and a reaction to the New York art scene's obsession with money and grandeur by peddling snowballs on a snow-covered street. It is referred to as a performance in hindsight, but it was also just a thing someone did because they wanted to.

In 1981, the French artist Sophie Calle was hired as a chambermaid in a hotel in Venice. Calle secretly photographed the belongings of the hotel's guests, used their perfume, read their letters, ate their food, looked inside their wallets and through their bins, and eventually presented her findings in a series of twenty-one voyeuristic diptychs. The artist was only able to make these intimate pieces because, in the role of a cleaner, she was completely ignored. Yet as an artist, Calle demanded attention, and her attention proved the power of the cleaner's gaze.

In the 2023 John Moores Painting Prize, the longest-running painting competition in the UK, one of the pieces selected for exhibition was made by Linda Aloysius. Titled *The First Painting in History to be Recognised by a Public Museum as Painted by a Working-class Single Mother Artist*, the work consisted of a used cotton tea towel hanging off two wooden spoons. In submitting the tea towel, the artist proposed there was a painting of her invisible labour in the house-hold stains picked up by the cotton; a portrait made not in the studio, but in the home.

In 2019, the artist and graphic designer Jon Edgley shared invitations online to his performance 'That's a Wrap'. With a tiled background of the hoisin and sweet chilli chicken wraps available as a part of Tesco's meal deal, the audience was invited to attend Edgley's last shift at the supermarket. He later framed his uniform and listed his four years on the job as a solo exhibition on his website. Edgley was commenting on the inherent performance required of public-facing workers, and also on the fact that artists rarely admit that their artistic practice is not their sole source of income, afraid they will seem less credible if they do.

In 2012, David S Gallant wanted to be a game devel-oper, but he was busy working in a call centre at the Canada Revenue Agency. So, he decided to make a short point-and-click game about his job. In *I Get This Call Every Day*, the player receives a phone call from somebody who wants to update their address. The game involves selecting dialogue options in order to take the caller through a series of tedious security questions, which the angry caller consistently fails to answer. Players expect games to be *fun* but this is frustrating in order for the player to empathize with David's real experience at work. After the game's release, which was shared with a pay-what-you-can price tag, his employer said that it was offensive, and David was fired from his job for making art as a way to cope with what he had to put up with.

Who Pays for Art to Happen?

To: BAFA LEVEL 3 (All)
CC: m.makin@csm.arts.ac.uk
From: q.talukdar@csm.arts.ac.uk
Subject: Please enjoy my bootleg notes

Hi everyone,

I went to that 'who pays for art to happen?' seminar they put on yesterday in a room round the back of the library that I've literally never seen before. I can't really believe it wasn't a proper lecture because it was the most important stuff they've taught us, and it's crazy that only 20 people could sign up. I've tried writing my notes as full sentences for anyone who didn't get a place (everyone) or find the room in time (quite a few people) and I'm pasting them below. I dunno if I remembered everything the tutor said but we graduate in less than a month so this email's gotta be better than nothing, and it's probably good for me to write the most important stuff they've taught us in a Word document and not on a loose piece of A4 paper I'm gonna lose long before any of this information sinks in.

CCing Mark so he takes the hint when he's putting together next year's timetable.

Who pays for art to happen?

Rich people.

Rich people bankroll artists directly by commissioning art or paying for an artist's living expenses (rare but does still happen. The tutor said sometimes celebrities keep artists like pets). Rich people also give their money to galleries, museums and prizes who distribute the cash for them by paying artists to exhibit, inviting them to speak, or buying art. Proper term for museums purchasing art is *making acquisitions.* Proper term for rich people who put their money into art is *patrons.* The tutor said if we look at the logos on the bottom of a press release or check the plaques in the foyers of museums, we can see who is paying for the art to happen. Some patrons might have their company's name listed instead of their own, and we can go on a .gov website Companies House to check who is running stuff if we wanna snoop.

Rich people also do *patronage* when they buy works through commercial galleries. Commercial galleries sell artwork on an artist's behalf. The artist has to make the work with their own money, but apparently the gallery is better placed to get that work in front of 'the right people'. Dealers, collectors, various forms of rich people. The gallery gets artists studio visits and art fairs. But if the artist sells something this way, the gallery takes a cut anywhere between 20 and 50%. I asked if it was even worth trying to get gallery representation, and the tutor said '20 or 50% of a sale is more than zero,' so that's me told.

Some collectors acquire works to donate to public collections (makes them look good), some have private collections (makes them look good), and some just wanna put things on the walls of their mansions (makes the mansions look good). Other collectors buy works specifically to sell them at auction later on when the artist is further along in their career and the work is worth more. Tutor called these people art investors. Sounds like rich people gambling. This example doesn't actually pay for art to happen, because artists don't tend to see any money when their work gets flipped on 'the secondary market'. She did say there was something called DACS – I looked it up after and it stands for the Design and Artists Copyright Society – and they have lawyers who advocate for resale rights. But generally speaking, it's not good news for artists.

A lot of it wasn't good news for artists, to be honest. The tutor said that patronage can be a way for rich donors to get good press and asked us to think about why someone might need good press. What are they trying to distract us from? She said, 'concentration of wealth doesn't happen naturally,' and then she said that high levels of wealth are only possible through the exploitation of someone or some*thing* somewhere down the line. She told us to think about bosses exploiting workers, companies exploiting customers, colonizers exploiting environments. I managed to write another quote she said, which was, 'accumulating absurd levels of wealth is always unethical.' There was a breakout where we had to discuss in groups how we felt about the fact that museums often work with unethical people, especially when artists work with those museums, and one day *we* might be those artists.

When we resumed, there was a slide on the presentation that said, 'if museums refuse unethical patronage, how do they expect to survive?' The rest of the seminar was about the word on the next slide, 'funding', but she kept saying that funding wasn't necessarily ethical either so it was a bit confusing. Instead of relying on rich people, if a gallery wants to pay their staff and put on shows, or if an artist needs money for materials, travel, research, there is something called a funding body. Funding bodies can be the charitable side of a business, or foundations set up by *dead* rich people who want the living to divvy out their bank accounts. All you need to do is fill in an application form to ask for some of the money they've got available. She showed us an example. It was a long form with sections where you could explain how much money you were asking for, what you were planning on doing with it, why the project is worthy, and who is going to benefit from the project happening.

The tutor said the biggest funding bodies are the ones giving out public money. We have something called Arts Council England. There's also an Arts Council for Wales and Northern Ireland, and Creative Scotland up north. Our one gets a chunk of its money from the taxpayer via the government. The rest comes from the National Lottery. I didn't know about this. The lottery gets so much money from ticket buyers that they have millions left over even after paying out the winners. They give out lottery surplus to sports and schools, and some goes to art. This sounded good in the same way it did when I was daydreaming a rich person might bankroll my every wish, but the tutor told us not to get our hopes up.

According to her, there is so much competition, money is limited, and success rates are low. She said they don't give the big-money projects to lone artists who need money to make art for their own satisfaction. They are more likely to go for projects that have a lot of 'public value', i.e. art that satisfies the public in some way. Like public money for public art. She tried to get us to do a second breakout where we were supposed to discuss the natural impulse to make the kind of art we want to make versus the influence funding structures have on what artists are paid to produce. But none of us knew what to say because we had only discovered funding existed twenty minutes ago, and we were all flip-flopping between getting really excited about the possibilities and freaking out that the art we made was never going to fit the bill.

I didn't make any notes after that. I kept thinking, is it too late to start a Third Year Fine Art lottery syndicate? Ay, at least when we lose, we'll still be supporting the arts.

Best wishes, or sorry for ruining your day,

Quest

The Q&A

'The kind of art I make usually gets written about as social practice. It is not my favourite phrase, and no one cared about it for a very long time. I was a player on the bench of a second-division team until galleries started getting in touch because they wanted to "work" with "the community".'

It was the first year of university and there was a full-length swimming pool built into the floor of the lecture theatre where tonight's speaker was floating on a lilo. The artist, Daisy, put her hand to her ear, pretending it was a phone.

'Hello, Daisy? When we wrote our last funding application, we said a few things we're a little worried about. See, we knew we had a higher chance of getting funded if we said that we'd do community projects with marginalized people. You can get us people, can't you? We think it would be so good if we could pay you to do that because we'll get to take pictures of these so-called minorities in our gallery and we can use those pictures to support our next application and we'll never have to worry about getting paid again. Kisses!'

She pretended to put the phone down.

'I am cynical, but that's how it is, and if you plan on becoming artists, you need to know what you're getting yourself into. Funders really love "people and places" right now.'

I had my feet in the water because the artist had welcomed us to sit around the edge of the pool during the Q&A.

A girl across the pool stuck her hand up.

'Hi, thanks for tonight's talk. I wanted to ask, if you feel cynical about this way of working, why do it?'

'Well, I make this type of art because I make this type of art. It's what comes out of me. It always has. I hate working on my own. If I have others to bounce ideas off, there's so much discovery and energy; there's serendipity and interesting comments in the in-between moments when people forget they're working. So that's reason number one.'

The lilo she was on bumped into the side of the pool and she pushed herself away from the edge.

'Reasons number two, and three, are that I don't trust galleries to do outreach, and I also don't think their mad desperation to get people is entirely their fault. Most of the galleries you're shown on a Fine Art course aren't commercial spaces that survive off sales. They're going to be galleries that have to go through the endless rigmarole of funding applications, and whoever's footing the bill ultimately gets to sign off on what a gallery puts on. When it's public funding we're talking about, galleries have to play nice, and seek to fulfil the aims of their local government's cultural strategies. That is where the cynicism really kicks in, because it's easy for them to dish out money to a few artists to make art about resilience, for example – make it look like they're doing something about our mental wellbeing or combating loneliness. But the government uses culture to fill the holes in people's lives, holes that have been made by the very government trying to half-heartedly fill them back in. That gets to me, because it's a lot cheaper to fund a brief art project that pays lip service to resilience and distracts people for an hour on a Saturday than it is to give people a robust Universal Basic Income, housing, food, therapy, healthcare, safe places to socialize, or anything truly life-saving. Free school meals. Free meals full stop. In other words, all the things that mean we wouldn't need art to teach us how to be resilient.'

She smacked the water.

'Funders want to back projects that are social and useful and good for publicity. But you know what was good for the public? Pubs, and they keep letting them close down. I heard the philosopher Mark Fisher talk about that at an event at Rich Mix years ago, how capitalism has utterly forced individualism on us. It's separated everyone violently so we can't discuss its effect. If we could get together, we might realize our problems are common problems that aren't our fault, even though we tend to blame ourselves, thinking we're the failures, *we* haven't worked hard enough. Capitalism wants us to internalize that failure because not only will we try working harder to get ourselves into a better place, but if we think it's our fault, we won't relate it back to the structures that keep us feeling like shit.'

Daisy found the student who had asked the question.

'I can't afford to be above the problem. I trust that I think deeply about this, and I've been doing so for years. Community is a beautiful thing that can exist quite happily without Fine Art. When art waltzes in with its own agenda, things can get prickly. But I am bound to the relational aesthetic industrial complex with the same commitment the government is to our misery.'

We'd learnt about relational aesthetics in a seminar. It was coined by a curator called Nicolas Bourriaud in 1998 to describe art concerned with human relations. He referred to the artists who worked in relational aesthetics as 'facilitators', and preferred the word 'artist' for someone who made work from their own imagination.

A student in one of the years above me asked if there was a way to make art *without* going to local authorities or funding bodies, but I didn't quite know what that meant.

'I'm seeing more artists ask their own communities to pitch in with crowdfunders. I'm a bit hesitant myself, but I suppose it's the same way I feel about charities; crowdfunders wouldn't need to exist if the government did its job. Most of our needs indicate something the government has failed to provide us with. We have to keep each other afloat. We have to advocate for each other. We have to show up for each other. I've been doing this for about twenty-five years now, so I've picked up loads of collaborators – and by collaborators, I mean artists I ethically align with.'

A boy in a cravat stuck his hand up.

'More of a comment than a question.'

Oh, here we go.

'An art practice is about the production of artwork. Social practice should not take up space in galleries when there are so many *visual* artists waiting for their time in the spotlight.'

The room was quiet.

'When I come into a place, I want to make art *with* people. Not for them. We work together to deliver what people feel they need from art. Not everyone feels like a painting on a wall is what they *need*, which is fair enough. I call myself an artist in rooms like this, but I am probably closer to an interpreter. I interpret communities for institutions and institutions for communities. That process also counts as working with people – working between them. Having to use those different languages of performative, official, professional artspeak. Being a "creative practitioner" when it holds more weight. Not mentioning the art at all when I know it would put someone off. I interpret art into real life, real life into art; bodies out of water, and finally back into them.'

Earlier in the talk, Daisy had spoken about campaigning to reopen her local swimming pool. She did it by gaining the support of patrons of the arts by persuading them a pool would do more for people than a one-time exhibition ever could. She said she hadn't got an artist fee for that project, if she could call it a project, because no gallery had commissioned her to do it. Nani had always told me that I should never ask someone about religion, politics or money. It wasn't polite, but those were like, the most interesting things about a person, and I needed to ask her what an artist fee was. Did she have to pay galleries a fee? That didn't sound right.

'The fee is the amount a gallery pays you for the job. It should never be the other way around. Artist's fee is a terrible way of wording it. Do you want to know how much I usually get paid?'

I nodded like my life depended on it.

'Commissions have been anywhere between two and four thousand pounds, and there is generally a separate budget for materials. Do you think that sounds like good pay?'

I had absolutely no frame of reference.

'OK, I can try to give you one. For the 2021 to 2022 tax year, the median annual pay for full-time workers was £33,000. Three grand is an artist's fee that comes up a lot when I chat to other artists and it sounds quite big, especially when it's coming in one lump sum.'

Especially when everyone I know is on an hourly rate of around a tenner.

'Say I do one or two projects a year, other years, none. I'd have to do eleven to land in the median, and that's literally never going to happen. A friend of a friend did a solo show at Tate Liverpool last year and their take-home was five grand – a Tate show is a once-in-a-lifetime job. We see it as the pinnacle of what we're all aiming for. But the numbers don't add up, and that's because artists being underpaid subsidizes the rest of the industry; the head of the Tate is on something like £170,000. Isn't that actually silly?[28] Talent gets paid the

28. *Structurally F–cked* is a 2023 report written by Industria looking into the working conditions of artists. The report found that artists were enormously underpaid, and that this pay inequality was a financial balance that kept the rest of the struggling sector afloat. It is available to read for free online.

least and the corporate structures around it leech off us.'

The person who had asked about cynicism very gently asked why anyone would be an artist given the structures Daisy was talking about.

'I'm not going to wait for someone to whip out the commission before I have ideas. I have ideas and I have an urge to act on them.'

She got off the lilo and out of the water. She was so nimble.

'Not to end things by stressing you out, but I don't think I'd be at all happy if I left art behind for a *proper job* with a *proper wage.* I've watched friends do it, and one of them isn't with us any more because it got to a point where he no longer had a relationship with his practice.'

The room was silent again.

'He never had luck with funding or galleries. He worked in a shop and he told me once that he felt like he'd lost his identity. It sounds over the top, but it so thoroughly destroyed the fabric of his existence to *live* the wrong existence. I get in my head about it, thinking he'd probably still be alive if there wasn't such a problem with how money is distributed in this country, where organizations are entrusted with huge amounts and we expect them to share it out with fairness in how they go about it. It doesn't *have* to be this way.'

She began to dry herself off.

'Compare it to our closest neighbours. When I mentioned Universal Basic Income earlier, I didn't want that to sound like politicians talking about a magic money tree. These things don't have to stay in the realm of our imagination, they are already in reality. There's a pilot in Ireland that involves two thousand artists being given €325 a week. It's taxable, and we don't know if it will last, but that's one attempt at levelling the playing field. If we travel a bit further, look at artists in Norway who can apply for an annual stipend. They call it a Working Grant, and it equates to around twenty-four grand a year, which is a bit more than the Irish equivalent. But the Norwegians can get it for five years. Back in the sixties, when Leo Castelli opened his gallery in New York, he had artists on payroll, which meant they made money even if their pieces didn't sell. In England, there's no longevity for artists. That's so dangerous.

'I've always liked the Artist Placement Group. That was the sixties too. Barbara Steveni was driving out to get materials from a factory one day, and she described it like a eureka moment, where she thought, *why aren't artists here?* What would happen if artists were placed in commerce, industry and even in government? She thought that if businesses invited an artist, *paid them*, and gave them an open brief, the artist could bring new ways of thinking that would benefit whatever context they were in. I love that because it is *applying* an artist's

103

work to that other context, and in doing so, revealing what it means to be an artist.

'Still, that's for the benefit of whoever's paying. I don't know if you've heard about what the MAYK Theatre is doing in Bristol. They hired three artists to get them off the "project treadmill" as they phrased it. One full-time, two part-time, they're getting twenty-seven grand a year pro-rata, and they're on PAYE, which means paid holiday, sick pay – a pension, which really is the holy grail for artists. They're not expected to end the pro-gramme with a fully formed theatrical production. Their time is up to them. They can learn, take risks. They can afford to make art that doesn't make them any money.'

Daisy had thrown clothes over her swimming costume while she was talking.

'Most artists can't afford to be artists, and yet, that doesn't mean you should stop trying. It is probably an irresponsible thing for me to say, but I do believe deep down that it's worth being skint and free, rather than a bit better off and suicidal. It is incredibly difficult to stay alive, and as a society we have tried to make all sorts of systems in order to deal with that difficulty, but they don't work for all of us. We have to come up with ridicu-lous coping strategies to stay. I live in a shithole, I teach three days a week, and I spend the rest of the week in the studio. You could argue tonight's £150 speaker's fee wouldn't feel like such an insult if I went full-time at my other job, but I would argue I might be dead.'

She pointed at the lilo.

'I'll leave this with you. The pool will be open all week, or until the next lecture. Use it however you see fit. Have fun. Relax.'

I felt buoyed by her, knowing that a buoy only just manages to stay above the water but some of it is always drowning.

Maslow

Throughout my time at university, and for many years afterwards, I worked as a caterer at Exhibition Centre London, which might sound like a gallery but it isn't even close. It's a very long, very wide hangar where businesses gather for home shows and retail expos, that sort of thing. I manned a burger stand that was too casual for the weekday crowd, which was fine with me. I spent my shifts pulling down the stiff arm on the side of a slot machine, applying for opportunities on my phone. Residencies in Scotland, Norway, South Korea, wherever. Online residencies too. A few alternative education schemes. Bursaries, commissions, competitions. I made myself a custom spreadsheet to track results. I thought, even if I got a no, I look forward to reviewing my own stats at the end of the year. My own Spotify Wrapped for applications. I wanted to see it as a continuum, so rejections never felt like dead ends, because writing applications did help me develop my ideas to some extent. I kept a column on the spreadsheet for the ideas I put in each application and made sure to recycle them so that I never had to work from scratch.

Everything, in and out of art, is a competition, so I thought I just had to get on with it. I tried to see writing applications as a *thing* I did. I made art *and* I made applications. If I was an academic or a poet, I'd be sending submissions to journals. If I was a journalist, I would be pitching articles. Maybe it was no different from that. I tried to be optimistic! But then I would imagine myself lying down on the train tracks in the trolley problem; if 1,000 people apply for an exhibition, but only ten get in, is the happiness and relief of the ten worth the misery of the rest? Of course not, and yet I would always find new tracks to lie across, and wait to see how the art world wanted me to feel.

I went to exhibitions even though I was tired. I saw a Ma Qiusha exhibition at Middlesbrough Institute of Modern Art. In the darkened gallery, alone, I watched *All My Sharpness Comes from Your Hardness*. The film, shot from above, shows the artist's feet dangling off the back of the car she is strapped to. She wears ice skates on her feet, which sharpen against the road as the car drives through Beijing. Sparks occasionally twitch away from the friction and I found the sound of the blades excruciating. The exhibition handout explained that Ma Qiusha was being dragged along the route she used to walk from her childhood home to her grandmother's. I looked up and they were my legs on the screen now, kicking and screaming, no elegance or control, begging the invisible driver to set me free at Nani's. *Let me stay there, let me paint. Let me go to bed when the sun comes up. I don't want life to sharpen me.* I wept alone in the gallery because I was afraid it already had.

I needed art to be under the impression I was good to go whenever, wherever, at the drop of a hat, on the back of a moving car. I had to hold on. Writing applications was a job in itself. Caterer, application writer – there was no room to be an artist as well. Nobody warned me becoming an artist meant filling in endless forms in a desperate plea to make art. Nobody had told me that I would be bidding against so many others hoping for exactly the same. If I had known . . . well, I wouldn't have listened anyway. I don't think I would have believed that art could be so dry.

With the last of my will, I went to Art Night when the festival had spread its arms around Walthamstow. I got caught in a stream of people flowing from Zadie Xa's performance in a library with orcas, dancers and watery lights; on to the market, for Hannah Quinlan and Rosie Hastings' pride float; and ended up at Walthamstow Trades Hall where Diane Chorley was singing, Oscar Murillo had signed up thirty of his own friends and family to boost the club's membership, and the audience had repurposed Art Night guides as coasters for pints of bitter.

There was a sign over the bar that said you couldn't hang about once you'd been served, so I found a spare seat on the edge of the dancefloor and asked an old man if I could sit. I offered him some of the crisps I'd bought from the bar.

'Man is a perpetually wanting animal.'[29]

He took a few, and introduced himself as Maslow.

'Are you one of these?'

His head jerked to the side and I nodded. The room was unusually full of London art-enjoyers, wearing wide-leg pants and Comme des Garçons Converse. I told him I was an artist, trying to be, and asked if he'd save my seat so I could get more crisps. I hadn't had any dinner.

'We'll have to get you fed otherwise you'll never make art again. If man's needs are not satisfied, then the organism will be dominated by its physiological requirements.'

I came back with a second packet, downed a lime and soda, and did one last trip to the bar for cheese and onion, salted peanuts, a J_2O, and then I was good. The singer had been replaced by the John Ongom Big Band, and they were loud, so I thought speaking time was over for old Maz.

'You know how to look after yourself. After all, you can't self-actualize if you're not taken care of.'

Self-actualize?

'You do want to be an artist, don't you?'

29. Abraham Maslow's text *A Theory of Human Motivation*, 1943.

I *am* an artist.

'Thought you said you were *trying* to be?'

I tried to let the saxophones drown him out.

'Well, before you can become what you are – before you can become everything that you are capable of becoming – you have to make sure all of your other needs are met so that you have the means to satisfy who you want to become.'

I held the nuts up with my bare hands. The nuts would satisfy me.

'Hunger is one of those needs, yes, but I'm thinking more broadly than that. After you satisfy your biology, you need to make sure you take care of your safety.'

I thought he was taking a paternal dig at me for wandering the streets of London alone and relying on Walker's for sustenance.

'You need to place yourself in an organized, predictable, familiar world – i.e. a good home – somewhere that protects you from danger, and also from extremes in weather.'

Before I fell down the floorboards, I complained to my landlord about the mould in my flat. In response, he sent someone round to install 'air bricks', which, it turned out, were gaping holes drilled right across the walls for ventilation and my own personal torture.

One of the many contributing factors to my miniaturization.

'Once the body and the living situation are gratified, man experiences new motivations. The need for love, friendship and belonging. Do you have good friends, young lady?'

I asked him what he was on about.

'I'm *on about* you. Your field. Community is a great foundation from which you can cultivate esteem, and we *need* esteem. Esteem from others and from ourselves – self-esteem, self-respect. It gives us confidence. Respect. Independence. Freedom.'

But I didn't have Comme des Garçons Converse.

'What I'm saying is there are certain physiological, social and psychological needs that someone needs to satisfy before they can entertain the idea of becoming who they really want to be. Pretend this is a pyramid.'

He took the three empty crisp packets and arranged them in a triangle between us.

'We have a calling in life to become someone. An artist, a good mother, a top athlete – whatever it is. But if the artist, the mother or the athlete has no food whatsoever – if they are dying from hunger – they'll be thinking about eating before art, children or exercise. The same goes for their safety. The same goes for their sense of society, and their esteem. It is a hierarchy of needs, each relying on the prior satisfaction of the other. At the very top of the hierarchy –' he put a peanut at the apex – 'is self-actualization. When everything else is satisfied, a new need emerges. What do you think it is that an artist *needs*?'

To make art.

'Precisely. If an artist is not able to make art, well, we can expect discontent and restlessness in the individual until he is doing what he is fitted for.'

I noticed there wasn't much room at the top of the pyramid.

This is why so many artists are rich. They aren't rich because they are artists, they are artists because they are rich. Rich people get to be who they want to be. The rest of us don't get to come close to the ultimate version of ourselves, so we put up with becoming the person we *have* to be. We don't get peace or happiness or fulfilment. We scrape against the road and sometimes there's a spark, but other times we die.

Realistically, I'm never going to live my best life or be my best self or make my best art. Fuck me for trying. To be honest, I don't want to think about that ultimate version – it's morbid. What's *more* realistic is the fact I am going to make art *anyway*. There are plenty of artists throughout history who didn't have a pot to piss in or a window to throw it out of, and those people offer empirical evidence that you don't need a perfect life to make important artwork that people will use as props in their arguments hundreds of years later. I'm not saying I am going to become someone art history remembers. I don't think art is this rare event that we only produce when the stars align. Sometimes the house opposite gets shot at but you paint a picture because it's what you want to do.

Sure, the starving artists might have made better work if they'd had salted peanuts from the bar, and the tortured artists might have made better art if they'd gone to therapy. But maybe not. Other artists say they make their most interesting work when they are at their worst. Make that make sense! Artists who take as their subject *the human condition* are thrown closer to their subject matter when shit hits the fan. Maybe I'm one of them. After the landlord drilled holes straight through my bedroom walls, I *did* use them for pinhole photography.

Back when I was at university, there were students who didn't even want the radio on when we were in the studios together because they didn't want it to give them a false sense of happiness in case it tricked them into thinking they liked the work they were making. Some artists don't want to feel good *or* bad. They want to be totally neutral, otherwise they cannot read their own work. I don't think I've ever experienced neutrality to know what that feels like. I can't imagine I ever will.

War of Attrition

In 2017, Tiona Nekkia McClodden put herself through what she termed an 'ordeal path' in order to honour the poetry of Brad Johnson. Responding to the love, desire and sadomasochism in his writing, the ordeal path saw McClodden reading the poems while tied up, cutting, limiting her breath, masturbating and being beaten with roses by a dominatrix. During these acts, the artist wore a Navy basic-training T-shirt which became marked with blood and sweat, to empathize with Johnson's creation of poetry aboard a Navy vessel. The Museum of Modern Art acquired McClodden's tribute, which included a video, hooks, chains, dried rose petals, and the T-shirt which held the artist's bodily residue. There were seventy pieces in total. But in 2022, a floor supervisor at MoMA binned the Navy T-shirt because they did not think it was part of the artwork. McClodden later made the difficult decision to endure the ordeal path a second time *to make the work whole again*.

In 2014, Hilde Krohn Huse was on a remote island in Norway. She needed a particular shot of herself hanging naked from a tree for a film she was working on. She tied safety knots, undressed, pressed record, hung upside down, and held her pose for the minute of video she needed. That's when she felt the rope tighten and the artist realized she was trapped, naked, alone, and cutting off circulation to her limbs. The performance was over. It took thirty minutes before Krohn Huse was found, although the camera cut off after eleven, by which time the artist was desperately shouting for help. Watching the recording back the next day, she realized she had a very different artwork from the one she had originally wanted to make – one that was so affecting because she did not seek the work, yet the work happened to her anyway.

The Canadian performance artist and bodybuilder Cassils set themselves on fire in a controlled stunt in front of a live audience. The title of the piece, *Inextinguishable Fire*, was inspired by the Harun Farocki documentary about the Vietnam War. There is a moment in the film when Farocki picks up a lit cigarette and says, 'a cigarette burns at 400 degrees Celsius and napalm burns at 3,000 degrees,' before putting the cigarette out on his own arm. In a separate performance, Cassils once froze their naked body against an ice sculpture of a man's chest for five hours, until their own heat melted the danger away.

The No-show

It wasn't that I had a bad reputation to give these people reason to reject me; rather, I had *no* reputation at all. I got jealous of the students I graduated with all those years ago who existed in the world as *real artists*. It was weird, or it wasn't, that the students who did well were the same ones who got the degree show prizes. A studio for twelve months, a residency in Florence, a £1,000-pound voucher for Cass Art supplies. I couldn't tell if they were the very best artists in our year, if the mention of an award on their CV had made that much of a difference, or if they were booked and busy *because* they got to carry on being artists when the rest of us had to get jobs. I wasn't jealous at the time. I honestly didn't think anything of it. But those three *prizewinners* got to stay in the specific dreamstate-headspace that art school had spent years seducing us into, while the rest of us had to quickly snap out of it.

Maybe I didn't have the right pictures. I was still making art, and it wasn't a diamond produced under huge pressure but more like the weeds that emerge through the cracks in the pavement. I'd tried photographing my weeds, but the only place with decent lighting was the kitchen table, which was set next to landlordcore beige

116

wallpaper embossed with flowers. I knew the people receiving my applications would want to see a high production value across the art and its documentation, because that would make me look like a high-value individual. I was going to need to take photos of my work in a way they would appreciate. I needed the art to look as if it was *already* on display; the same way adverts for razors show women shaving hairless legs. I needed the particular staging of the white cube.

I'd started getting books out of the library for the first time in years, probably because going back to university didn't seem possible. I was scared about what might happen if I got myself into any more debt, which is something that didn't used to affect me, but I could feel myself becoming more brittle. I'd been reading the work of Irish critic Brian O'Doherty. He wrote about the strangeness of the white cube format, and it excited me because good writing laid out the problems impeding art in a way that reminded me I wasn't alone in facing them.

The white cube is a modern gallery style that curators like to see as a neutral space for experiencing art. I have found it jarring ever since I was little; cold on the palms of my hands, and my feet. But I didn't think that reaction was allowed. I thought that if I wanted to be an artist, I had to be OK with every single dogma of its faith. The premise of the design reminded me of transubstanti-ation: Catholics believing a prayer turns a wafer into Jesus's body; curators believing that four white walls, sealed windows, no frames or labels, summons the ideal gallery into existence.

The white cube is where 'the sanctity of the church, the formality of the courtroom, the mystique of the experimental laboratory joins with chic design to produce a unique chamber of aesthetics'. Brian wasn't much of a fan, and I could see why. By denying the outside world's presence in the gallery – by removing all evidence that art is, in fact, just a thing someone made – the white cube frames artists as bizarre aliens and artworks like impossible treasures. With no evidence of the real world, only a maddening inertia remained; like the lighting in 24/7 windowless casinos, I didn't like what that meant for the audience. When I was in front of art, I wanted to connect with it. But in the white cube, I felt like an intruder as soon as I arrived. I was not sterile. I must be exorcized by the architecture before I am allowed to view the remarkable pieces on display. The fire extinguishers were silver so that danger no longer existed, but neither did safety in that equation; I couldn't photograph my art on the kitchen table because it revealed too much humanity.

I'm sure I used to enjoy going to exhibitions. Every year, an art fair takes place in Regent's Park under a colossal white tent like a forensic team erecting a shelter over a dead body. I went along to one to see what it was like, and I watched a man approach a painting with a measuring tape, shake his head, and ask the gallerist if it was possible to trim the sides off the work so that it would fit

into one of his alcoves. They got straight into negoti-
ations and – was that what I was working towards? I
would speak to Brian in my brain. *Brian, are you still
there? Can you hear me? I don't want to be the body
under the tent who is chopped up and sold to strangers.
I yearn to be an artist, but, Brian, it is starting to hurt.*

I'm sure I used to enjoy sharing my art. I posted bits and
pieces on Instagram because there was nowhere else
for it to go, and also because I didn't want anyone to
forget me. But with the white cube so pervasive in the
minds of powerful art forces, I couldn't understand how
it got a pass when it came to social media; I'd open the
app and see someone-I-didn't-know's dog had died,
someone-I-went-to-school-with's baby, then there might
be a painting, but it would be sandwiched between a
horrific news story and a gym progress pic. I didn't want
my art in and amongst that shite. Did that make me a
snob? *Oh God, Brian, none of this feels right.*

I'm sure I used to enjoy art. On the weekends, the
business conferences at work were replaced by con-
ventions. Huge queues of fans would arrive early so that
they were first on the floor. In a sense, the cons upset
me more than the endless keynote presentations.
Anime, drag, soap operas. I could never get over how
many people congregated to celebrate the art they
loved. Fine Art was too uptight for the warmth of
fandom. I wish it wasn't. I wanted merch for Lubaina
Himid. I wanted Beatlemania for Bhupen Khakhar. I had
always felt love for art and found that there was

nowhere to put that love. Applications weren't loving. Rich people weren't either. Money was hateful. The white cube was cold. I wondered why I bothered making art if there was nowhere safe for it to go.

I realized I was invisible when I snuck out the back to smoke, and my manager also came outside, called his girlfriend, and proceeded to bitch about the entire team right in front of me. I was stunned. I waved a hand in front of him to remind him I was right there and – nothing. I went to snitch on him but found that no one else could hear me, and I didn't even feel sick. I felt free. I walked into work the very next day with a suitcase and a ciggy in my mouth. I'd had an idea.

Mum had been calling me quite a lot to check in lately. Must have known I was losing the plot. I went on a date last week but the girl was a no-show, so I told Mum it had gone *really well.* She was doing an MA in Art History at the Courtauld. She listened to the *Einstein on the Beach* soundtrack and liked contemporary art that recalled the classical: Michaela Yearwood-Dan, Marijke Vasey, Philip Williams. She wanted to collect them one day. I couldn't tell if this character was someone I wanted to meet or someone I wanted to be. But the more I lied, the better I felt, and Mum was very impressed.

It was fun trying my imagination on again, like an old coat that had fallen down the back of the wardrobe. I think I'd forgotten artists could lie. Lies are what I'd brought with me in my suitcase. I'd wrapped the biggest sculptures in moving blankets, and the fragile pieces inside cotton wool and Tupperware. I had a camera and a tripod in there too. Exhibition Centre London had endless spaces in all shapes and sizes and I knew where to find a room with white walls and a severe floor. I knew which storeroom to pillage for the plinths that clients sometimes used to showcase brochures. I pocketed nails, a spirit level, a hammer . . .

I was going to build myself an exhibition that no one would ever see. I took a wide shot of the whole room once everything was in place. I took close-ups. I photographed the show from every angle and set a timer so that I could position myself with my back to the camera. A visitor deep in thought. I took my jacket off, tied my hair up, and took another set smiling at my imaginary photographer. Artists always get a cheery photo at their own show. I spread some press releases around the room, too. I'd taken a leaf out of Wills' book. I was sick of the perfect set of circumstances that only supported a few, and when I put my finger on the scale for a split second, I felt the blood rush back into my body.

I took my laptop out of the suitcase to clean the photos up and I uploaded the best ones to my barren website. I decided to say the show happened last year at a space called the New Arts Gallery – if anyone ever bothered to google it, the words were generic enough they'd never catch me out. I sat admiring the new exhibition page like I was somebody else seeing it for the first time. It reminded me of holding my very first paintings up to the mirror on Nani's landing; I hadn't realized how important that step was until I could finally stand back and *see* what I had made, something I hadn't been able to do when all of this art was stuffed underneath my bed. It was transformed once it was dusted and on display. Transubstantiated, even. I could look at the sculptures from different angles and see how pieces worked in relation to each other. I could also see what I'd change. Taking the artworks through the process of exhibition, documentation and publication gave me a sense of completion, as well as new direction. I almost wished other people could come to my no-show. That date I made up. Mum.

If you're going to rob something from the supermarket, why waste that risk on a banana or a loaf of bread? Why not steal the most expensive thing in the room? Why do we not think we deserve to? While I was still editing my website, I gave myself an award. Remember those residencies in Scotland, Norway and South Korea? Yeah, I made it over after all. I also mentioned an upcoming show, *details to be confirmed, by appointment only*, and I posted the updates to Instagram. I realized I could turn the lights off, project a single image on the wall, photograph the projection catching the slight grain of the wall, and blag I'd made an entire film. A short film, a long one. I could write down whatever running time I wanted and only I would know the truth. So I did it, I gave myself a film.

'Oi! You're not allowed to smoke inside.'

I wasn't so invisible any more.

Good Liars

For five months in 2014, Amalia Ulman's Instagram page documented a young woman moving to a new city, experiencing a break-up, doing drugs, getting a breast augmentation, drinking, recovering, and falling in love again. The 88K followers she amassed in that time had no reason to suspect the validity of her posts, but the entire story arc was a carefully devised performance. The artist once wrote, 'In this world where everything is fiction, the best story wins.'

In 1991, Suzanne Treister created a series of fictional videogame stills on her Amiga computer using a program called Deluxe Paint II and photographed the images directly from the screen as if she'd seen the games in an arcade. There are fifty-five stills in total. Stills, dreams, lies. The graphic paintings depict mazes, ladders, ketchup-red fire extinguishers, and choose-your-own-adventure text boxes. One game asks: Have you been sentenced to a fate worse than death? The player has no way to respond.

In 1998, William Boyd wrote a biography about the late artist Nat Tate. He asked David Bowie to write something for the blurb. There was a party for the launch of the book at Jeff Koons's studio where Nat Tate's paintings were hung for the occasion. Guests spoke fondly about the artist's life, rest in peace, etc. But Nat Tate wasn't real. He was the invention of Boyd and Bowie. He was the National Gallery and the Tate combined. The pair interrupted the routine of high-class culture, and the launch party took place on April Fool's Day.

In 1961, the Italian artist Piero Manzoni sealed ninety tins of freshly preserved *Merda d'artista*. Artist's shit. The work came after he sold balloons inflated with the artist's uniquely commodified breath. In the year 2000, the Tate purchased a single shit tin at auction for £22,350. No one knows if the tins contain real out-of-his-arse shit; Agostino Bonalumi, one of Manzoni's friends, said it was plaster. The buyers don't really want to know, because as soon as they open a tin to check, they will tank the value.

The Real Artists of Beverly Hills

This bleak shit is how I ended up in business class. On the way to LA. The present-tense panic attack. Right, I told a few lies here and there about exhibitions I may or may not have been in – victimless crimes – and lying got pretty addictive, or effective. I don't know how guilty I should feel about that. I want to be an artist. Mum said I could grow up to be whatever I wanted to be; school said all we had to do was go to university; university said stick together and see where life takes you. Things had not been going to plan, and I was stuck doing an irrelevant job that used up all my time and energy. I don't feel shame in coming from a normal background where I have to work for a living. It's more that, practically, I just have to do a lot of that work to afford to live. If there was a way to make money really fast, that could free me up to spend life like I wanted to . . . I was going to have to get creative in how I made my money. I was going to have to start telling bigger lies.

This industry didn't function in a sensible way, so I wasn't going to be sensible any more.

I kept a tab open for Contemporary Art Daily, which shares pictures from exhibitions all over the world. I needed to know what was trending. I had another open for Sotheby's auction house to study the market. I combed through K-HOLE's trend forecasting predictions. I found a rise in items that hinged between artworks and products; Platform Art were selling a $200 vegan-leather yoga mat designed in collaboration with the cartoonist Robert Crumb; I didn't even do yoga and I wanted one. I was convinced I knew what was coming next for our collective fragile psyche.

In my madness, I mostly went on Instagram. I followed artists who were getting attention. The theory seemed to go: successful people had the most followers and the people with the most followers were successful. I didn't like a lot of the art that existed on these pages but that didn't matter. Images with bright colours were sticking to the top of the timeline and I realized I was going to have to appeal to magpies by making art that was *beautiful.* The most-wanted, the most conspicuous. I also noticed that the most-liked images weren't only showcasing art. There was always someone in the picture. That was annoying. I didn't want to be a part of this if I was going to have to make art I didn't even like. I was a normal person who bought make-up from Superdrug. I wasn't the right person for the job.

The solution needed to be some four-quadrant shit, easily appreciated by the biggest cross-section of people, and that wasn't me – brown scouse artists aren't exactly flooding the market. Maybe it could be somebody else. I had to create QT. Don't get me wrong, I love my name. Quest Talukdar sounds like futuristic software. But no one would ask me how to pronounce my name if I went with QT. Plus, it sounded like *cutie*.

I took wood from one of the skips round the back, I bought cheap neon paints, and I made huge pink-and-orange paintings. I left a blank body-shaped space in the centre of each painting where I imagined influencers might stand, pose, dance. Outfit of the Day. I hoped the paintings could double as seamless paper backdrops; a bit like the photo-spots that shops, restaurants and bars had been fitting over the past few years to massage everybody's ego while giving themselves free advertising. They didn't count as real art, these were potboilers – easy, likeable things an artist makes purely for money; to keep the pot boiling. They were like hotel art or restaurant art. Something to give the periphery a touch of colour so that a room feels more complete. I'd gift the first few to influencers with significant followings, and maybe they'd post colourful squares with white bodies front and centre, and hopefully they'd tag me and . . .

I couldn't make the big shit neon shit quickly enough. The gifting had worked. Microinfluencers started buying the paintings because they wanted to post content that looked like it came from the professionals. Then, the interior design accounts clocked on. It moved off Instagram. Stylists wanted the paintings for props. Pinterest helped me out. Blogs followed. The works were welcomed by the visibility industry,[30] making paintings that required people to include themselves in the documentation. Next-gen photo stand-ins where the participant gets more attention than the art. If I sound like a snob, I don't mean to. I felt a twisted solidarity with the people buying these paintings. I bet you influencers have panic attacks all the time. It is crazy that they have to make people *like* them for a job. It's actually sociopathic to have to build your own cult following so you can capitalize on people's love for you. Not that dissimilar from the art world, really.

I was creating a system for myself. My hope was that QT would fund a more avant-garde practice. I could use the weekends to produce these bullshit paintings, and the rest of the time, I could be making the real stuff. QT could get me to a place where I didn't have to think about money, I could finally think about art and only art. Allure made up for the quality lacking in the art – influencers stood in the way so you couldn't even see how bad it really was. Without a face to the name, absence of context gave me glory in the white cube, and as the legend grew, the enquiries grew with it. To uphold the mystery, I invented a studio manager who

30. A term Gabrielle invented to refer to the manufacturing of well-known people whose visibility allows them to promote things, influence people, and generally profit off of their own visibility. See: industry plants. See: buying followers. See: the sale of ring lights in the phone repair shops on every other street in England.

would reply to emails on QT's behalf. I felt unstoppable speaking in another person's voice. I called my studio manager *April Furst*.

I was flying under the race radar with the help of default Simpsons-yellow emojis. And maybe this is bad of me, and bad for representation and all the rest of it, but there was something of a relief in deleting my own identity. Between galleries in England dying to be seen as inclusive, and the infographics I scrolled past with carousels of 'Five Inspirational British South Asians You Should Know', I could have manipulated my art so that it was hyper-Asian. I understand museums are under pressure to show fewer David Hockneys and Peter Doigs, but the way they go about finding *us*! Every time I filled in an application form, I had to tell a stranger whether I shagged boys or girls, and where I was at with my gender, and I had to give them my Ancestry.com log-in, and tell someone my horoscope, and the occupation of the highest earner in my household when I was fourteen years of age, and let them know which foundation shade I went for and whether or not I got cold sores – and a little bit of me died.

I watched friends apply for opportunities that were predicated on identity, but if their art wasn't as noticeably trans as somebody else's embroidered pink-, blue-and-white flag, or as obviously Black as somebody else self-portrait, the gallery didn't want anything to do with them. Not only did the gallery want Identity-artists, but they wanted Identity-art; the gallery wanted everyone to know that they had Identity-friends. It seemed very much about advancing the gallery, and not the artist; and I didn't want to contribute to a competition that had more to do with *who* I was, as opposed to what I could *do.* I believed the consequences of identity were too complex and too tender for us to be working these things out within earshot of the British Empire – I mean, the British art scene. I didn't think I should have to. I just wanted to make money so that I could make art. If the art world wanted to know exactly who I was, then I wanted to be no one.

The only problem was, I was having non-stop panic attacks. I was charging *so* much money for cheap acrylic paint slathered on thin wood, pure matter, and each one only took fifteen minutes. I *had* to exploit other people in order to gain my own freedom. There was no ethical consumption under capitalism, and I couldn't think of ethical ways to *earn* money either. I was coming up with new colour combinations based on trend cycles. I was doing fast fashion. The artist Marcel Duchamp once said, 'abundant production can only result in mediocrity,' and I was banging them out abundantly. The work appealed to the middle. It was acceptably boring. But I think that's partly why I was having panic attacks; I didn't get into art to be boring. The whole point was that I was going to do something emotional and irrational and new.

The scheme was only working so well because buyers didn't care much for ideas. That is terrifying news to anyone who wants to be an artist. Art puts forward the idea that you are free to do whatever you want. But the artists who tend to sell are not the ones who have complex knowledge to offer, or complicated sets of interests or histories. Commercial galleries want something that's easily consumable. They want drive-thru art. Something you can do yoga on. The institutional art world *does* want ideas, but they won't pay nearly as much as the gallerists, dealers and art fairs. I had to choose between making money and making work that I was actually interested in. There was no scenario available where I got to do both. Not even this, whatever *this* was.

If anyone caught me, I was going to tell them QT was an act of institutional critique. QT was a performance that sought to undermine the art world's obsession with accolades. QT had no shit to can, no air to blow, no body! QT was a post-racial, post-gender, post-demographic puppet! If only I liked QT's work. It was awful. I liked artists' art that was very different from market art. Fuck the neon paint burnt into my retinas. The edges of my fingernails glowed like I was radio-active. I hated the days I had to go to my studio to make more of the neon shit because I was jobbing it now. Wow, I couldn't even enjoy finally being able to afford a studio.

Whenever you start doing anything professionally, it becomes a different entity. I was both my boss and my worker, and the workday alienated me from the art I produced. The sales alienated me further, as did the emails, as did April Furst, and the factory-line production of paintings that were bulletproof products in a way that art should never be. It wasn't art that was coming from somewhere animalistic and vulnerable inside of me. Nobody who knew me could ever find out what I had become.

Mohammed

I reckon this awkwardness around art started on that cursed Friday back in school. I was happily minding my own business, painting a lake in class, when Mrs Kelly leant over my shoulder and said that my lake looked like soup. *Apparently* I couldn't put it in my portfolio – the one I was applying to universities with – looking like that because the paint had gone *muddy*. Oh no. Muddy meant what I was mixing had become too grey, too brown, impure, desaturated.

Mrs Kelly didn't suffer fools, so I tried my best not to be one. I hung on to her every word. One Monday I came in with a painting I'd done of Nani's front garden. She asked me why I'd chosen to paint it, and I told her, well, I thought it was nice.

'Nice isn't enough!'

I wanted to be a part of Mrs Kelly's world where *nice wasn't enough*. I loved the way this woman saw art. I was in love with the way she spoke about it. I know she was only one of my teachers, but out of all of them, I really wanted her approval. She had a way of thinking, and a shape to her thinking, that I wanted her to imbue me with. She knew loads, not just about art. She had an openness to the whole world and everything inside of it, and she spoke with a curiosity that I didn't hear in my other teachers, which made me excited for university.

I'd had my reservations about getting into debt to 'learn art', which felt like this intangible talent that people were either born with or they weren't. But Mrs Kelly showed me that studying art meant learning how to interact with the world and with each other with a very special sensitivity; to her, art wasn't about making nice pictures, it was an interpersonal skill that you could practise and use to interrogate your relationship with the world. My art teacher showed me how to paint lakes, but she also taught me how to be a person.

So, she could call my art whatever she wanted. I would never be offended. The pupils in our school who were planning to go to uni tended to apply for things like Biochemistry and English. Mrs Kelly needed this win. Don't tell her this but in my head I called her my Art Mum.

We were at the beginning of a double period on a Friday afternoon when she made me pack up my belongings and went all jingle-jangle looking for spare change in her massive patchwork tote bag. *Apparently* I was getting the bus to the museum. *Apparently* it was 'the only way'.

'If you want to paint water, you need to observe how artists have painted water in the past. They solved the riddle before you were even born. Take Mohammed with you.'

I cringed. Mo was my boyfriend. We had been going out for a grand total of four days. He was the only other person wanting to study Art. He was in the middle of one of his big, intricate collages when Mrs Kelly roped him into my artistic development and he looked openly annoyed. I told Mrs Kelly that if she named the paintings she wanted me to look at, I could google them.

'Don't be ridiculous. When you're doing a degree – a degree I will have helped you get on to – are you going to tell them you'll *google* the paintings? You're too comfortable in this classroom. All of you. Learning isn't supposed to be comfortable. Mohammed, get your coat. I don't want the school suing me if Quest goes missing.'

He told her she'd get double-sued if we both got kidnapped. She said she'd take the risk.

'*How* do you like this *shit*?'

Mo had his knickers in a twist.

'Honestly, how? 'Cause I like art but I only like makin' it. Galleries – ahdunno.'

On the bus in, I told him that me and Mum came here loads in a bid to hype it up, but I might have gone too far. He was standing in the middle of the permanent collection with his hands behind his head, groaning like he already wanted to leave.

'Shall we jib it?'

Knew it.

'We've been here ten minutes and I've forgot what the point of a museum even is. That arl woman looked at us like we had a cheek comin' in 'ere. She must have shit herself seein' two brown teenagers walk in. Getting stop-and-searched just so I can look at a paintin'. I am norrin the mood. How am I supposed to *look at art* after that? I feel like I'm the one they wanna look at.'

I didn't notice the staff when it was me and Mum walking round, but there were staff circling the two of us in the gallery, and Mo didn't care if they heard him.

'And then what was it, chargin' us seven quid *each* for the exhibition. Like we have exhibition money. We're literally in school uniforms. An' all I said was can you say the artist's name again. Not my fault I dunno who they are. I dunno anyone. I never come 'ere. Then he speaks to me like I'm soft. *Well, the permanent collection is free.* Well, *thank you, kind sir.* I am eternally grateful for these still-life paintings and the endless portraits of white people I don't know. Such an *honour, your highness.*'

I was a bit entertained, a bit uncomfortable. I felt like a pushover for not expecting a better customer experience, a better visitor experience. I didn't blink when they stopped us at the door. Was I entitled to more? Maybe it wasn't that deep. Or maybe I didn't think I was entitled to walk in without a pat-down because I was a lowly commoner. I thought, I should probably start thinking more of myself soon, or the rest of life might be up to other people to decide.

Mo carried on taking the piss.

'Welcome to our gallery where we showcase the things that white people once owned. Their kids, their naked wives, their houses, their dogs and their fuck-off massive fields. But don't get carried away now, this collection only covers the nice stuff amongst their belongings. We don't want people to shout at us. No, no, nothing bad happens here. If anything bad did happen once upon a time, something that might have involved our Great British country messing up other people's countries, or people owning other people, for instance – we'll do our best not to remind you so you have a lovely visit looking at ten thousand paintings of horses with funny-looking legs.'

He was being quite loud at this point, and it made me nervous. I was also mesmerized *because* he was being loud. As for what he was saying – Mum always said if we don't like something, keep going until we find one thing we do like, because there's always something. Mo seemed to be under the impression the museum wanted to impress him with every single thing it had to offer. I wanted to tell him, it wasn't the whole museum you had to like. You didn't *have* to like any of it.

He sat down next to me with a thud.

'How is this the only bench? Urgh, it's fine. I would rather sit down than carry on pretending to care. It's like, picture, picture, cabinet, picture, picture, read the card next to it, realize I don't get what it's going on about, try to read it *again*, not get it the second time either, carry on. It's so awkward. It's boiling as well. Are you hot?'

I was but I couldn't take my blazer off because I was very much a teenager.[31] Mo was talking faster and faster, and tugging at his collar. I thought we should probably leave. Mrs Kelly would be none the wiser. Plus, I could take my blazer off in proper ventilation (and Mo could stop spoiling my favourite building in the world).

'I've only seen two other people come in and both of them were on their phones. The man didn't even look at the work with his own two eyes. He had the camera open and he was lookin' at the screen instead of the actual, big thing he was a metre away from. I bet you he never looks at those photos.'

Mum always told me off for that.

'What's the point?'

Museums kept art safe. Their pieces were valuable or delicate or important and it wasn't like there were spare copies in the back.

---

31. She smells.

'Is the "permanent collection" genuinely permanent?'

It had been that way for as long as I could remember.

'But I don't get it. Why do you come here *all the time* if it's the exact same stuff on the walls? An' when there's . . .'

He got up and marched around.

. . . 'thirty-three paintings and two sculptures crammed into one room I can't concentrate. D'ya know why they've hung so much stuff up? Most of it's too high on the wall to actually look at, an' the stuff at eye level has shiny glass in front – which I get – but the reflection means I can't *see* the pictures without . . .'

He was going side to side, up and down, taking different angles, trying to beat the light.

'The higher-up ones are pointless because you'd literally need a ladder to look at the water in that boat painting. Who is it by? Thomas . . . Miles . . . Richardson. I'd be fuming if I was Tommo. Imagine his ghost coming for a gander an' not being able to find his boat painting that he spent ages on, because he floated round the room but never looked up.'

He looked at me suddenly.

'Wait, do you think the permanent collection is bad on purpose so you *have* to pay for the main exhibition? That's arlarse.'

He laughed at his own conspiracy. An invigilator shushed him and he looked at me like she had proven his point. I dunno. I kind of wanted to put my hand over his mouth too. I know Mrs Kelly said learning shouldn't be a comfortable experience, but this was shit; I'd never had anything against the museum, but I didn't completely disagree with Mo, and that concerned me.

'I swear, everyone who works here thinks they're the police. Can you give these people a review? I am gonna give them a one-star rating. Swear down.'

Me and Mum had so much fun when we came. I told him how we played: which one would you take home, where would you put it in the house? We'd try to find friends and family in the portraits. We'd guess how much stuff was worth . . .

'The money one I could go for. They should have the prices next to the paintings.'

But people wouldn't be able to see past the numbers. I didn't wanna know, the same way I didn't wanna see calories next to food items on a menu.

'Maybe people shouldn't be trying to see past the numbers . . .'

An invigilator shushed Mo *a second time*. He shushed her back. We looked at each other and ran.

'Sorry. I'll shut up next time.'

In the daylight, I thought about what I was going to have for tea. The best bus to get home. Normal, straightforward things that had no hidden agendas. No loaded histories that personally alluded to my place in the world on a cellular, social, financial or cultural level. I wasn't ready for *this*. I wasn't ready for Mo. I wanted to like what I liked without second-guessing myself.

'Come with me.'

I didn't really want to. I wanted to skip the gallery and go straight to the kids' playgroup; I wanted to shrink back to a time when my life was nothing but art and instinct. The trip had achieved nothing besides making me realize that when some people went into a museum, they couldn't feel anything other than stress.

Mo led me round the corner where the museum backed on to the river. He apologized again. I'd wanted to see art through Mrs Kelly's eyes but now I was seeing it through his. He walked me to the railings and told me to look down. The water below us was muddy; the River Mersey wasn't blue, it was brown.

Valentine

We broke up. I don't want to talk about it. We were together for the rest of sixth form, but I chose Fine Art at Central Saint Martins in London because it gets mentioned in that song 'Common People' by Pulp. Mo went with Painting and Printmaking at the Glasgow School of Art because he had an aunty in Scotland he could live with for free. Fine! We were meant to go on a big romantic summer Interrailing trip but I went alone with a backpack, pepper spray and a cob on. I felt like Marina Abramović and Ulay when they walked from either end of the Great Wall of China and planned to meet in the middle to get married. But it took them eight years to secure permission from the Chinese government, by which time they didn't even like each other any more. They still did the ninety-day trek but when they met in the middle, they said goodbye instead, flew home separately, and didn't see or speak to each other for twenty-two years. Yeah, that, but I was doing the walk on my own.

I kept my camera around my neck in case I saw something that looked like the sort of thing an artist would pay attention to. I was desperate to be interesting. I was desperate to become an artist, whatever that looked like or meant. I went all over and by the time I reached

France, I was so busy panicking about my lack of talent that I wasn't thinking about heartache any more. The old woman who ran the hostel in Paris asked me if I was OK. I explained that I was about to study Art, but I wasn't actually any good. Every single photo I'd taken looked like one of a thousand postcards you could buy on the street.

'People want to see something they have not seen before.'

The woman in the hostel grabbed a pen from the till and took one of those maps for tourists off the counter. She scribbled for a moment before rotating the paper.

'This station here – take the train to this stop. Behind is a valley. There is a château. They say it is bad luck to take a picture of the château. The local people will not do it. But you are not local.'

If I arrived at art school with a picture of a forbidden place that even the locals would not dare commit to imagery, then maybe I would seem . . . deep? Forbidden places could even become my *thing*.

'I think about it sometimes, you know, because I met a man in the valley a long time ago. Must have been your age. A little older. He was an artist like you – oh, I loved him. I have no picture of him *or* the château to guide you. Only the memory.'

She started writing something else on the back of the map. I recognized the address of the hostel.

144

'If you find it, send me a picture. Let me know if he is still there.'

Afternoon was becoming early evening in the damp valley, which *was* beautiful, but in the picture-perfect way that postcards are. It wasn't going to work. There were no houses on hills, only butterflies and normal flies and me in my wet Vans. I took one final picture of me in front of the landscape so I had something to show the aunties when I finally got home. I looked through the viewfinder to get everything straight, held my breath, and made myself as still and solid as possible. It took a second for the image to load on the screen but when it did, I thought the isolation or the break-up or the pressure of being eighteen years old had finally ruined me.

In the picture, the valley was there, but there was also a huge, old stone house. I'm sorry, what? I zoomed in. Tiny little raindrops popped against the screen. It was more like a *castle*. I moved the camera out of the way to find that a house had appeared out of thin air.

It started pelting down so – not my best idea, but – I walked straight up the hill to knock on the medieval door. No answer. I knocked harder and felt it push open a little. The rain ushered me in and the wind closed the door behind me. It was pitch-black. I swung my backpack round to the front in a bid to find my phone for a light, and as I dug my hand in – I heard footsteps and breathing and somebody approaching and I screamed and I fumbled and I shot the pepper spray and *a man screamed*. The darkness got even darker, and that was it. Instead of dying a dramatic death, I fainted out of pure fear.

I woke up on a chaise longue in a large room with a fire blazing in a huge fireplace. It was old-old, like walking-beyond-the-ropes-at-a-historical-houseold. Speke Hall interiors.[32] Thinning carpets, cobwebs, my chair was upholstered in a fabric that looked centuries out of style. The only not-old things were all the paintings leaning against the walls. They were covered in faint shapes. I thought I could see constellations in them.

'There you are.'

I jumped.

'I'm really sorry for shouting – and for giving you another fright just now – I hope you're feeling better. I don't get any visitors out here.'

There was a man sitting in a deep-buttoned armchair next to the fire. He was pale, thin, sharp jawline, dark curly hair. Mid-twenties, French accent. He was wearing a black velvet suit . . .

I took over the apologies. I was intruding. I was also attacking. I started rambling in an attempt to explain myself. England. Art school in September. Here on my own but please don't kill me now that you know that.

32. Speke Hall, a Tudor manor house in Liverpool, 1530–98.

Don't know what art to make. There was this woman – she told me there was a bad-luck building in a valley that I should take a photo of. Was this the building? It certainly felt like bad luck.

I made to leave.

'Oh, go if you must, but you are welcome to dry off here, wait out the storm.'

When I shifted my weight, I heard my shoes squeak. He gestured at the seat opposite. I looked at his face properly and he was smiling to himself.

'Of course you're an artist. How else would you have found this place? I am an artist too. That's actually why I'm here.'

The paintings were his. They were spilling up the imperial staircase. No imagery, only celestial, empirical geometry; spindly lines, metallic dots, and shaded angles done so carefully that they must have had an internal logic of their own. They reminded me of sundials – and left me wondering how somebody could ever figure out this shit with no computers. Wrangling space and time into such intricate human measurements. Was this his studio?

'Yes. I do also live here. I moved in a long time ago. The place belongs to my family. It's special. Protected, I mean. It's cold but it's perfect because . . . I get to be alone. It's what I need for my work. You know, I would tell you to do the same – to find somewhere like this where you can create – except you are so young. I shouldn't say these things. Or you shouldn't hear them. Not yet. Your heart is still opening, and evidently doing so with enough vitality to come to places like this in the middle of nowhere, all in pursuit of an image.'

He spoke carefully, lyrically. I didn't really know what he meant but I was smoothing my baby hairs back. I couldn't believe he lived here on his own. No wonder I'd scared him. *Why* was he alone?

'I don't want to say these things to you when you are on the cusp of so much. You'll be meeting your tutors and peers and soon enough the unexpurgated *art world* and its population. But that was the problem for me: other people. I knew from a young age that I was an artist and, like any young person with the same predilection, I assumed a career in art would be focused on art. I was wrong! It was . . . social! It was all about people!'

He made a face like he'd smelt something bad.

'Meeting them, speaking to them, performing for them. Listening to their opinions. Holding up my own opinions for their inspection. I suppose you would call that networking nowadays. Everything, always, *people*.'

He began pacing in front of the fire.

'No one ever spoke about art. They only spoke around it. They spoke for the sake of speaking. I wondered if it was *my* fault – if it was too hard to speak about the work I was making, because there was nothing recognizable in the paintings for these fools to label. But then, it wasn't only my work. No one would look art in the eye, and it made me feel like a madman, and a misanthrope.'

Oh no, did I have a thing for men who complained about art . . .?

'I endured people for long enough. I was never going to bow down to the kings and queens of art – I am French after all. So, I made my escape. I wanted perfect silence. I wanted isolation and it needed to be total, all-encompassing and permanent.'

I laughed nervously because I had ruined his permanent silence but he thought I was laughing at him.

'I'm being serious. I like it here. I'm not some Holden Caulfield, Heathcliff-style loner, pining for company. I'm not oppressed by circumstance. I'm Citizen Kane in Xanadu. I'm Elvis Presley in Graceland.'

I pretended to get the references.

'I needed to be alone so that I could finally make art.'

His paintings were bigger than any I'd ever seen before.

'You see, there's this apparent, necessary truth that everyone buys into – that being an artist involves being part of a *community*, as if that's of inevitable benefit to your work. The fact that those *communities* are full of insufferable, self-important people with nothing useful or interesting to say never comes into it. Forging a life as a professional artist is an incredibly difficult, almost chance event. You would think artists who felt the impossibility of that would want to help each other. But I only found people pulling the ladder up behind themselves. Where did that leave me?'

He paused as if I actually had an answer for him.

'No, you shouldn't think about other people. They shouldn't even cross your mind. You should only be thinking about your art. I left, and there are no ladders here. No snakes, either. This is my small utopia.'

I asked him if I should cancel my plans and move to a château in France. You know, if he could bear to have me as a neighbour.

'I shouldn't have said anything. You have to go through these things so that you can decide for yourself what matters. I let myself be exposed to art's regime and it burnt me; the rest didn't realize they were on fire. Good for them, I suppose.'

We were both quiet for a while. I had a question for him, but I didn't know how to ask it without sounding judgemental. If I didn't, no one else would. So I asked him if he was OK.

'I'm better than I used to be. I was going mad out there, constantly interrupted by nonsense that I did not want to waste a minute more of my life on. I don't go mad here because . . . well, I make art every day. It helps that I have my family's generational wealth, a body that never falters, and it also helps that I am responsible for nobody but myself. I don't keep up with the news. I really have no idea what goes on outside of these walls. I don't care to. I wish every artist could access an oblivious state like I have.'

It seemed polite at this point to tell him how good his paintings were, but he stopped me. He didn't want to hear it. Good or bad. I had to keep my opinions to myself.

'Oblivion.'

I froze.

'I know you didn't mean anything by it, but I don't need a sounding board or praise or complaint. It's not neces-sary, nor is it desirable. I think it is an imposition on artists that others feel the need to offer input on their decisions. What does anybody else know of my heart? There is an aspect to an artistic practice that marks the externalization of something internal, but I am happy to externalize that to myself without having an audience in the room with me while it happens. It's a process of self-reflection, almost like a tic – a nervous, psycho-logical tic. I need to get the art out of myself one way or another by drawing or painting or any other method by which the material becomes *done*. I absolutely do not accept the requirement that somebody else should validate the material in order for the art to reach that point.'

I went to open my mouth and he put a hand up.

'It's when I *do* start to notice that imposition pressing upon me – the imposition that my art is for somebody else – that I lose interest. I am prone to anxiety about other people's judgements, and I would prefer to imagine that I live in a vacuum in which other people's judgements are irrelevant – *or* in which I can decide those judgements myself. Imagine that. A situation in which not only do I create the work, but I also judge it under my own terms. An alternative reality in which my work *is* presented to people, and I can fictionalize how they react to it. As a framework, such fiction would be a great deal easier for me to handle. Maybe you're not real. I made *you* up to tell me my paintings are *good.*'

But how does he *know* whether—?

'I look at it. Common wisdom would have you think that other people's opinions can dramatically aid in the development of an artwork. That's why critics exist, isn't it? But criticism is a second-order activity akin to sniffing bicycle seats. It's something people do for their own pleasure in the absence of the creator they're actively speaking of. I'm extremely *for* criticism, but amateurs shouldn't attempt it. I'm interested in the opinions of people who really know their field, and that's as true of criticism as it is of the weather forecast. I don't want to listen to rubes.'

I think I was whatever that meant.

'As an artist, my general feeling is: *leave me alone. What's it got to do with you?* If you want to see what it is I've done, by all means, peer over my shoulder. But I can only do the thing that I do, and the moment I have to filter that through the opinions of others, I can't allow myself to care because the art changes into a second-order thing, *like* criticism – and also like writing that has gone through an editor, or art made in a university that has gone through *group critique*.'

I'd heard of group crits and I was very, very scared of them.

'Then don't go to them. It's only necessary to meet a desire in yourself, whatever that happens to be. Other people's desires are their own responsibility, and you can't account for those. But then, I've always been self-sufficient. To answer your question, I know if a work is any good because I know whether or not it ends up in the bin. It's like anything – if you're a baker, you bake ten loaves of bread and one doesn't make the cut. You trust in your own professional understanding to make those decisions. You don't put the loaves in a room and invite fifteen other bakers to offer their opinion. That's ridiculous behaviour. Other people's opinions can introduce a new set of doubts which have no foothold or relevance to an artist's thoughts; and there are enough elements of doubt naturally built into the artistic process. If you rely on the *curse* of other people, then your artistic practice – which should be yours alone – becomes nothing more than a *group project.*'

He moved his shoulders quickly like he'd got a shiver.

'Art is an intrepid and necessarily solo pursuit. There is an aspect of art practice, regardless of whether it's about the creation of *the thing* or the understanding of *the thing* or the communication around *the thing*, that *the thing* controls. That thing, whatever it is – the art – you simply need to be a conduit for it. That's complicated enough without having to also accept that *everybody's looking at me while I'm doing it.* That's impossibly stultifying. I'm interested in the experiences, opinions and work of individuals who believe wholeheartedly in the art they make. If you have to throw your art open to committee, I don't get why that should be of interest to me. While you're looking at me like that, I should add that I don't think being a reasonable person makes you a better artist.'

Maybe I died when I hit the bricks. Where was I? What time was it? Who was this man? What was his name again?

'Sorry, my name is Valentine. Yours?'

He asked me to excuse his bad manners. He was out of practice when it came to the art of hosting. When he left to get a bottle of wine from the cellar, I was glad of the break.

'I'm sorry. Art is the most important thing to me, and I know you must be excited to enter this new phase of your life, one that will bring you closer to art. It really doesn't matter what I say unless, in years to come, you need these words to matter – to give you permission to extract yourself. You shouldn't listen to people as old as I am, though. I have no idea what the world is like any more.'

I had assumed, or hoped, that Valentine was maybe five or six years older than I was, but the fire and the wine were blurring his face.

'Artists should make what they want to make. That's all.'

I started welling up. I told Valentine that becoming an artist still seemed like a hypothetical, distant event. At the same time, it seemed promised, like a birthmark or an occupational surname or death. I *knew* that art was there inside me, but I didn't know what to make. Worrying the birthmark might just be a smudge, I pointed at the paintings that leant against every wall of the château and said, *how do you make so much?*

Valentine reached over and took my hand in his. It was surprisingly cold given we'd been sat by the fire.

'I don't get up in the morning and think, what am I going to say today? I just talk, and so do you.'

Oh.

'Don't think so hard. Do the thing. Do the thing *even if* it comes out and it's not something you want to own. Look at it and accept that you made it. It *is* what you want to make, even if you think it's a mistake. It has happened. There it is. If you don't think you want it, you're wrong, because it's right there. *Then* you can start working on whatever it is you need to do to turn it into something that might get *a good mark*, or into something *a buyer* might want.'

He was being sarcastic, but it did make me laugh.

'I do wish you weren't putting this pressure on yourself. This is the other factor to consider with the education you are entering, that it will put arbitrary deadlines on your thinking. Art should not come with deadlines – I don't think a practice has any time attached to it. You're only going to university *now* because you are finally an adult in the eyes of the state and that means it's their first real opportunity to exploit you, starting with debt. After school, you become a worker in their eyes to start paying off that debt. School is fast and art takes time. It plays with time. It is strange to put an otherworldly practice inside such limiting structures. When you get to art school, they should give you your tuition fees back as vouchers for the art shop and say, *see you in a couple of years. Go and be a mystery!*'

I blinked away the tears, taking snotty gulps.

'*Be a mystery to others. Be a mystery to yourself.* How can you make someone else understand what you've made when you sometimes cannot even claim to understand it yourself?'

Valentine's eyes misted over, moony and brilliant.

'But that's the beauty of art! That's the essence of it, and what we must spend our lives searching for. How precious, to be able to make something that defies even your own understanding. For art to happen in spite of you. How divine it is to wrestle a power beyond the limits of your own comprehension! To forge something out of that chaos, that mystery and mess. To transform something, and have it transform you in return.'

It was the happiest I'd seen him all night. I dropped Valentine's hand and wiped my eyes. He took himself seriously, and I was going to do the same. I had taken my own opinions seriously before. When I was a kid, I could look at art, take note of what it did to me and believe in that without question. He caught me stifling a yawn and he left to fetch me bedding from the eighteenth century. He pulled the chaise longue forward so that I could sleep in the warmth of the fire.

'Take care of yourself. That's all I meant.'

I lay back on to the pillow and Valentine leant forward to place a blanket gently over me. For a second, through a gap in his shirt, I saw something on his chest. Black letters, a sentence tattooed in cursive. I asked him what it said and he undid the rest of his buttons.

'"A man's work is nothing but this slow trek to rediscover, through the detours of art, those great and simple images in whose presence his heart first opened." It's a quote from Albert Camus.'

I couldn't imagine Valentine lying politely under the lights of a tattoo parlour, so I decided the words appeared on his body when he needed them most.

In the morning, I folded the blankets and walked out into the valley without once turning around. On the train back to Paris, I took out my camera and looked at the simple image in whose presence my heart had first opened and I knew I couldn't show this to anyone. When I got back to the hostel, the old woman asked me if I'd found him. I shook my head. She said she thought his name might have been Valentine.

Do Not Disturb

Henry Darger was only ever known as a hospital janitor until his landlord discovered a 15,000-page book that Darger had written and illustrated, on clearing out his room. The book, *The Story of the Vivian Girls, in What is Known as the Realms of the Unreal, of the Glandeco-Angelinian War Storm, Caused by the Child Slave Rebellion*, features panoramic watercolours of euphoric, imperilled, sometimes naked children who episodically vanquish evil. The term Outsider Artists is used for artists who are self-taught, or whose private work is not seen until after their death. *The Story of the Vivian Girls* has the exact sensitivities that might prompt an artist to keep their work to themselves in case other people jump to conclusions. Darger's mother died when he was four; he struggled through orphanages, and was placed in an asylum at a very young age. He had one friend, a dog, and a lifelong desire to create art in which children vanquished evil.

In 1970, Adrian Piper drenched a shirt in white paint, hung a 'wet paint' sign around her neck, and walked down busy Manhattan streets. Instead of painting a canvas, she painted herself and, still wet, a work in progress, and white for now – Piper is Black – the artist was both a spectacle and a hazard that threatened to vandalize other people if they brushed up against her. She made herself formidable in an ordinary space, and did what she wanted to do without being deterred by what other people might think.

The cover of every issue of *Flash Art* says it is 'The World's Leading Art Magazine'. In 2008, the Austrian artist Maria Anwander spent three months meticulously erasing all of the images inside issue 259. A year later, Anwander went in with chemicals to erase all printed matter from another issue, including the text. In doing so, the artist questioned the power of magazines in the cultural industry, where editors and writers take their positions as our tastemakers; platforming, analysing and obsessing over a select few, while the majority of artists are never given the time of day. Anwander's erasure of the magazine's content is an act of silencing the loudest voices in art. It also kicks the pedestal out from under the idea that artists should have to rely on critics for a sense of importance and relevance – all artists are worthy, even if nobody has written about them, and even if they don't want to be written about.

The Group Crit

That autumn I stood in a circle with my new tutor group for our first crit, or that was the plan. We were at a complete standstill fifteen minutes in after listening to a sound piece. Not one of us dared to speak.

'Are we really going to stand here and say nothing?'

I stared at the speaker on the floor and pretended to think really hard.

'Say what's on your mind. Go on. It's not fair on Calum. They're sharing something and you're giving nothing back.'

Nothing, nothing, nothing.

'Anything?'

Nothing.

'Everybody grab a chair.'

Calum didn't exactly look ready and willing to receive feedback. They looked like they were going to vom.

'I haven't taken First Years for a while. I forgot you need easing in. Your art teachers probably showed you the colour wheel and maybe vanishing lines.'

How dare she belittle Mrs Kelly. But yes, true. She never touched on *boring sound pieces.*

'We do some technical stuff here. But at degree level, we expect more from you. The *art* expects more. It's like this, right. Today, you'll each present something you've been working on. You can give an introduction to the work if you want and tell people what it's about, what it's made of, how you did it. You can ask the group what you want them to consider while they're experiencing the work *or* leave it up to them. *That* can be a useful way of checking whether an audience reads the work the way you want them to.'

I don't think Calum meant to bore me.

'Your peer group is your audience and you should make the most of that because an audience isn't guaranteed outside of art school – some cultural industries pay for critical attention because they understand how important it is.'

There's no way people hire mute students to stand in circles in the real world.

'In theatre, a director looks to a dramaturge, whose job is to see if the director is getting their ideas across the way they hope they are. Game studios have Quality Assurance who play-test games right through production so that designers know whether the game is playable or fun or scary – or whatever the desired effect is. Comedy hires punch-up writers to keep a script snappy. Artists use crits. Say you get a *bad crit*, and you feel like everyone has read your work in completely the wrong way –' unless Calum *meant* to bore me? – 'well, then at least you know you need to tweak the work a bit more. Crits might teach you that clarity in art is really important to you. Of course, you might not give two shits about what the audience thinks. *Death of the Author* and all that.'

Not one of us knew what she was talking about.

'Ah, First Years. "The Death of the Author". It's an old essay from Roland Barthes. 1960s, I think. He wondered, once an artist has put their creation out into the world, is the artist's intended meaning more or less important than the audience's interpretation of it?'

Was Calum as bored by the work as I was?

'The crit is a testing ground for art, but it is also a *training* ground for the artist. On days like this, you can begin to consider your position on these broader philosophical questions. That muscle gets worked in crits, and you'll need your strength because art is philosophical; it's about existing, thinking, feeling, meaning. Art is lawless, and it has to remain so in order to open up new channels of understanding. That's what I mean about needing strength, because you'll want a shared language between you to debrief, or to help you move forward, when art leaves you lost for words.'

163

I would have been up for saying something to break the tension, if the first thing we'd been shown had given me one single positive thought.

'Once you get going, you can agree on what words mean between you. There is plenty of vocabulary to choose from. Does the artwork come off as deadpan, abject, sincere? Does it feel rooted? Is it spatial? Sound can be spatial, paintings can be lyrical, and sculpture cinematic.'

We all took notes. Deadpan, abject, sincere.

'If a work is slick, is that repellent to you, or infatuating? Sometimes the production value of an artwork is palpable and obnoxious. When a piece looks cheap, I've heard students use words like "pathetic", "scrappy", "twee". If a work is unimaginative, we might say it's "prosaic". If a work is made with traditional processes, with traditional subject matter, we might call it "atavistic". If an artist has made a sound piece using a collage of pre-existing sound pieces in order to make a comment on the place of sound in art, we might say it's meta-textual, or it's a caricature, or they're working in pastiche. This might sound like a foreign language right now –'

I didn't have a fucking clue what she was saying.

– 'but fluency will come with time and participation, and you shouldn't overthink it or you'll never start. Try giving your first impressions, which might be along the lines of

I like it, but I think it would work better if . . . In my experience, students tend to evaluate art based on its technical proficiency. I've heard people say, *those brush-strokes have such a confidence to them* – I've heard myself say things like that. But there's also the opposite of confidence, when you can feel a weariness to a piece, where it doesn't quite seem as though the artist has pushed it far enough and, as the audience, we don't even see it as a fully fledged artwork yet – only a sketch, a study, a prototype or a maquette, because we crave the next version, which we believe will be so much more complete.'

I liked imagining Calum's next piece. It took the pressure off today's crit.

'Does the piece remind you of anything? A lot of crits begin with students making those kinds of connections. Calum's piece brings to mind the soundtracks Ryoichi Kurokawa creates to accompany his light shows, where data is shifted into another form, and sound dips in and out of lowercase. Once I make that connection, I can present it to Calum. It might be helpful for them to go away and research how Kurokawa fills vast spaces. That might be something Calum wants to try out?'

Calum shrugged.

'I liked the piece, anyway. Maybe you didn't. That's a real possibility in a crit. You might hate someone else's work or, worse, they might hate yours.'

Oh God.

'But who gives a shit? The conversation is about *art*, not about *you* as a person. If you confuse those factors, you'll end up attaching your own self-worth to the successes or failures of your artworks, and trust me, you don't wanna do that! It'll stop you from taking risks in case someone judges you for it. Experimentation is too important in the development of an artwork, and accidents sometimes produce the best results. I want you to remember that opinions aren't facts. By all means listen to people's comments and their reasoning, but if everyone in the room thinks your art is shit, you don't have to suddenly believe it's shit. Their feedback is still important because it's there to remind you that your opinions don't define the work. Even though you're in charge of the art you make, you're not in charge of how your art is received, or understood. Learning that lesson, in my experience, can be quite liberating.'

I wouldn't want anyone to *control* the way I felt about a piece of art. That would leave nothing in it for me.

'If Calum's sound piece had ended and someone had said they thought it should have been twice as long, but Calum vehemently disagreed, the disagreement would have been a productive one because they would have realized length was an important factor to them. They can go back to the studio and spend a bit of time thinking why that's the case. The crit can identify which

strands of the work you could be experimenting on –
maybe try a shorter version?'

I wish.

'There will be times when you can't see a work for what
it is because you will have been working flat out to a
deadline, probably alongside jobs, or you'll have other
things on your mind to do with families and relationships. But you've got crits with people willing to help
you help the work along. You don't have to do it on your
own. I know artists struggle with this because they feel
that the work is less *theirs* for having the input of others.
But your art will be richer for having been worked on by
a full group of artists who want to see you succeed, and
that's *got* to be better than one person's singular vision.
It's just good to establish some ground rules before you
get stuck in, like you might do in a group therapy
setting.'

She thought for a second.

'I like Thomas Hirschhorn's critical workshop "Energy:
Yes! Quality: No!" He's a Swiss artist. He believes we
shouldn't speak about art in terms of *quality* because
quality is given its importance by cultural gatekeepers
like curators, collectors, critics, academics, magazine
editors and historians, and so on. There's a whole jury
to decide what counts as *quality art*, and in making their
judgement, the jury excludes everything else as not
being good enough to qualify. Hirschhorn sets out the
idea that it's difficult to connect with art on the basis of

quality alone, because what the fuck have the jury got to do with your connection to a work? When you walk through a museum, you accept that the art has quality because the art establishment has decided it's important enough to be in a museum. But you might stand in front of what is considered a very important artwork and feel nothing at all. The *Mona Lisa*'s boring. Hirschhorn thinks we should talk about art in terms of its *energy* instead, because energy is *always* applicable. It's like when little kids scribble on paper and their parents think it is a masterpiece. It has no quality whatsoever – no critic would bother reviewing it. But it holds so much energy that the parents keep it on the fridge for ever. When Thomas Hirschhorn runs one of his crits, a piece of art is placed in the centre of the room. The artists then take turns saying whether or not they detect energy from the piece. They simply admit to their own personal response in the form of a yes or a no. That's how it goes around the circle – yes, no, yes –'

No.

– 'yes, no, until everybody has spoken, and then there's a second go-around as each person explains their answer. Every time I've followed Hirschhorn's framework for the crit, the discussion has flowed.'

She looked at us hopefully, and to be fair, I was excited. I felt like she had given me a dare.

'Right, then, no excuses. Offhand comments can often be the most influential. Listen. Make notes. Roll with the punches, and realize they're not even punches, and that's the wrong figure of speech. You're here right now so *use* each other.'

We got back into the circle.

'Calum's piece has finished playing. You're all brimming with comments. You've got reactions and impressions and references and when I click my fingers, you're going to say them out loud . . .'

I said I thought the work was boring and the *entire* group breathed a sigh of relief.

Uncertainty

I came to imagine the art world's government as a claw
machine in an old funfair; rigged, overpriced and not as
much fun as it looks. I'd been a toy trapped at the
bottom of the pile and QT had dragged us out of the
dark. I felt the claw's metal arms closing around my
wrecked body when it plucked me off the plane and
dropped me into Frieze Art Fair.

I saw QT's initials in vinyl on the wall. QT's terrible
neon paintings hung over-electric blue carpet. A man
wearing massive gift-shop-jewellery rings on his
fingers. A woman with a long belted cardigan talking
about putting a piece on hold. One of mine? There
were Deutsche Bank logos. Figurative ceramics. Lots
of artworks involving mirrors and – there was also a
man coming towards me. He looked ecstatic. I
should probably be ecstatic; I have gallery representation and I'm in LA. But if nothing sells, I don't make
any money and neither does the gallery. I need
good luck, caffeine for the jet lag, and – this man
was still heading straight for me, and his hair was
long now, and he told me he was there as a writer, and
it was –

Mo?

First boyfriend, Mo. Mohammed, Mo. Broke up at the end of sixth form and I didn't even internet-stalk him because I didn't want to know, Mo.

'Didn't know you were going by QT now. Cool. Cool. Gonna have to change ya name in me phone.'

I pushed Mo out of the booth, out of earshot of the unsuspecting gallerist, muttering that he had me confused with someone else because my name was definitely April Furst.

'April Furst my arse.'

He still had my number? He asked me what was wrong, and I wondered how he knew to ask. But if I had looked through the mirrored artworks, I would have seen myself wearing a cheap polyester blazer and shaking like a dog next to ugly paintings that Mo really thought were mine.

There wasn't any food in the fair but we found a company distributing activated maca mesquite walnuts. Neither of us knew what that meant because we weren't American, so we sat outside under the shade of real palm trees, and it reminded me of the old times – Mo totally relaxed and me sweating in formal wear.

'Quest, what's going on?'

I could tell him that I had to make stuff up because if I could tell anyone, I could tell Mo. What I said was, art was supposed to be a beautiful human practice. Something we found pleasure in. Life was supposed to be

easier than this. It costs *money* to *live*? Mo, I fell
through the floorboards. I saw a gallerist kill and *eat* a
man. I became invisible. My art tutor was a mountain.
Of course I created QT. I had to. I didn't know that if
you wanted galleries to pay you, you needed enough
money to handle them not paying you well, or regularly,
or at all. I didn't know you had to be enthusiastic about
performing your identity if you wanted to secure
precious opportunities; I didn't know I would have to
redirect my art practice to fit a brief dictated by
somebody else's mysterious agenda. I don't want the
threat of an opportunity to determine what art I make. I
want to make my own decisions! I thought that was the
whole point of art? Becoming who I was always
becoming, not who someone else wanted me to
become? I had to create QT in order to make my own
opportunities. I think that's fair enough. Don't look at me
like I've gone mad when one half of the art world values
aesthetics over ideas and comes up with shit like art
fairs, and the other half values ideas over aesthetics and
is stingy as fuck. *Museums* are supposed to be the
ultimate destination artists are aiming for? What if I
don't enjoy them? What if I haven't enjoyed museums
since we went looking for paintings of water in 2012?
The world is always interfering and, for once, I wanted
to take charge. So no, I'm not QT. QT is a device
through which I make money, and that money frees me
up so that I can finally be the artist I've been meaning to
be. I have the job I want, *artist*, and I am doing the work
of *making art*!

172

Mo was quiet for a long time.

'I do sometimes imagine – I dunno why – that I've committed such a batshit, heinous crime that I have to go to solitary confinement. Leave me on my own with no one else, and I think I'd be all right under the circumstances because at least the writing would take care of itself.'

Oh, thank God, he got it.

'I mean, I'd be crazy, obviously. It's the naive dream of someone who hasn't ever been in prison.[33] But I think at the moment, the amount of human contact I'm obliged to have by virtue of my job is more than I'm capable of having.'

And what job was that?

'I *think* I am a writer. I thought I was an artist, but I like writing about art more than I like making it. The magazine has me travelling all over to interview people,

33. She didn't bring it up because, quite frankly, she was going through it. But at this moment, Quest had a passing thought about Wendy, who used to tell everybody she'd been away on her holidays. Much later on in her political education, Quest would think about Wendy again, and about how, below the working class, there was the criminal class. Criminality is not a gross moral failure but a systemic social failure. For Wendy, life outside of prison meant entering survival mode because the city did not provide for her in the same way that prison did. When she was 'on her holidays', Wendy had her basic needs fulfilled.

so that ridiculous prison fantasy is more to do with me imagining a world without work than it is me wanting to get away from people. It's me rewriting myself into a world where my desires are fulfillable, both because I'm the only one in it *and* because my desires aren't for anything that isn't already geared towards myself – only to the writing, which I can take care of by going inwards, not outwards, for features and interviews and all this shite.'

He sounded different, and I think I liked his long hai—

'Quest, you don't look well.'

I'm fine.

'What you were sayin' then, it sounds like you're accepting the rules of the art world without question. Or no, you *are* questioning them, but you're going about things as if the rules don't apply to you, instead of asking more interesting questions, like, *why are there any rules at all?*'

(Was Mo a theory bro?)

'Have you read 'Uses of the Erotic' by Audre Lorde? Or anything by Bataille, Georges Bataille?'

(He was, oh my God.)

'You sound married to the idea that being an artist is a job and the product of that labour is *artwork*.'

But art *is* work. We shouldn't undermine it.

'Dunno if I agree with you on that one. I think it's unfortunate that there's a linguistic connection between art and work and artwork. It makes it sound as if those things must be interlinked. We're so work-ish, psychologically speaking, and we have been that way since prehistory, that it's impossible for us to conceptualize anything outside of that framing. But take Bataille, right.'

What the fuck was going on?

'He has this conception of human consciousness that I chime with, where he says that people live in a kind of non-existence before work becomes apparent in their lives.'

Back when we were kids in class?

'Before even then.'

Back when I was a baby crawling round the museum.

'Yeah, spewing up in the baroque room.'

Getting burped in front of the Pre-Raphaelites.

'A non-existence isn't a bad thing. It's about a connection with the universe. Bataille says that it's work – the forcing of the self to do things other than those things that it would want to do – that is the source of everyone's problems. That's when consciousness becomes divided from the self. Work then becomes the thing you need rationality for, and you need perception for, and you need a sense of self for, *so* that you can perform work. He defines work as being an obligation to do things you don't desire, which I think is a massive problem for art because art itself is a very desirous act. It doesn't sound like QT makes art. QT makes work. I'm not convinced those two perceptions can be dissolved into each other. I don't think they *should* be. The world of work would love it if we desired work but we don't – it's the fucking worst – we desire an end to work. You and me, we desire art instead.'

I was buffering.

'Show me the actual art you make, because hopefully this QT palaver is worth the hassle.'

I blinked at him.

'What?'

I didn't have anything to show him.

''Kinell.'

The panic attack on the plane wasn't out of guilt for pulling the wool over a few rich people's eyes; it was because my life had become overrun with production, administration, accounting, marketing, managing the studio, postage and packaging. I kept telling myself I would quit after a year, but then I moved into a nicer flat, and – it sounds stupid but – I bought a nice couch on finance, and a roomy fridge, and those were two things I had always wanted. My monthly outgoings became so much higher that I had to carry on with QT's business because everything cost more money, and then because QT's sales were higher, it cost more to produce the work and –

'This is what happens. The financial system tells you to earn more money, and do less and less of what you really want to do with your life, and there are temptations in that system. Because in going up the ranks and earning more, you build an infrastructure around yourself that costs a certain amount of upkeep. So then you *have* to go to work because you need to afford all the things you said you were going to be able to pay for, like the couch and the fridge, or a mortgage and car payments and insurance and a funeral plan. Once you're in that life, of course, it's going to seem impossible to leave.'

I don't know how to get out. I don't know how to get to a point where it's acceptable to put my own desires before work, given the nature of those desires.

'Right? Because when desire is detected, a huge machine gets built around it that takes the form of the art industry or the music industry or publishing, fashion, games, film, telly – and the machine extracts desire from talent, and we have to let it happen, because we live in a world where talent isn't allowed to come into fruition without the very cynical support of capitalist machinery.'

QT isn't a critique of capitalism, QT is performing capitalism.

'Bingo.'

How do we get to keep desire for ourselves?

'Anarchy.'

Well, that was easy.

'If only.'

I stopped him before the conversation went any further because I didn't really know what anarchy meant.

'Oh, don't worry about it. We've got to a point in culture where we talk about intersectionality very casually, but political ideology isn't mentioned alongside race, gender, ethnicity, sexuality, disability and class, which is odd because political ideology has so much to do with the decisions we make.'

I wouldn't know what to call my politics. Coming from Liverpool, I voted Labour because that's what everyone did.

'Well, coming from Liverpool *as well*, I wouldn't vote for any of them. They're all gobshites. Anarchism is a distrust of authority. It's a political philosophy that imagines you don't need permission to do things. You can just do them. In fact, you can do whatever you want as long as it doesn't exploit another person. It's maximum freedom with maximum equality. That's the life it promises. A life in which your needs are met by your community, and your community's needs are met by you; and where that community is your primary social obligation, because there would be no welfare state to rely on. As it happens, there would be no state at all.'

He wasn't serious.

'Why not? I know it can be hard to imagine an anarchist world when this one ends up heavily overwriting the other possibilities for human existence, so it feels like there's no space left to be anything other than what we already *have* to be – those very few things we're told we *can* be. But I can try to imagine it for you, if you want?'

He took my hands under the palm trees.

'Close your eyes.'

He was very still; I was not.

'Anarchy could give us a world that focused on *being* as opposed to a world that focused on production and consumption. A world in which there would be no obligation to work. Nothing but interaction, and it wouldn't be an interaction like we're having right now, because this is so *stressed* – hiding in the shadows of an art fair, of all places, while you make these confessions and I try to make you feel better about them. Nah, we would be having interactions that were built on our entire lives as people who would have always done exactly what they wanted to do; because we would have been socialized in a way that encouraged that. That notion of "want" itself might even be a function of

179

the society we currently live in because we don't get what we want and consequently we want it.'

He was quiet for a moment but I kept my eyes closed.

'I know people are put off anarchism because they think it's this really teenage affectation to not want to go to work; it's also compounded by the fact that everybody has already been made to hate people who *don't* work, even though working conditions are often so unendurable for the workers that they would rather go on benefits, so how fair is it to hate them and their refusal and their imagination for another way of living? The hate is tactical. We don't want to be hated, thus we try to convince ourselves we *love* to work. But even if we got rid of work and money, there would be roles that people took on of their own volition, such as teaching and nursing and farming, because there's a satisfaction that we get from those actions that isn't financially motivated.'

Mum would still feed kids, I know that much.

'The best dinner lady I ever had.'

I'll tell her you said that.

'When it comes to art, the way I see it, if you lived a life in which your internal desires were met – and I'm not talking about the necessity to make an idea into its physical equivalent, but just to *be* that way and to *live* that way – then I think that *way* of living would become the art.'

He squeezed my hands and we both opened our eyes. I wanted to close them and go back into his description. Mo was making me homesick, and not for my flat in London, or my big couch, or my fridge. I was homesick for a world that didn't exist. Maybe that's what people should be referring to when they talk about *the art world.*

'Yeah, this isn't an art world we're living in, it's an art industry. You know, I'm surprised you didn't become a full-on performance artist.'

Why?

'Performance art might be the closest we get to art that's about *being* as opposed to *producing*. From your own account, you sound like someone who thinks a lot about how weird it feels to be alive.'

That's my favourite *and* my least favourite thought to have.

'Do you know Tehching Hsieh?'

I laughed, because I remembered a time before Mo knew the names of artists.

'You know how people used to punch a card into a time clock when they were going in and out of work? He did this piece where he punched into a clock on the hour, every hour, from April 1980 to April 1981. It amounted to a whole year of sleep deprivation for the sake of this performance, and I think about it all the time, because that one piece focuses in on how we decide to use time, or rather, how our use of time is decided for us. In giving himself absurd rules that he didn't *have* to give himself, it shows how absurd all the other *rules* are that we automatically live by. There could be a totally other way of organizing life that doesn't end up in the subjugation of the working class. This current organization of society doesn't have to be permanent, but we aren't prompted to think those thoughts or imagine things otherwise, so we go around *not* thinking about how mutable life really is.'

He really put himself through it.

'Sometimes I get nervous when it comes to anarchism because the transition from this life to that one would probably involve so much discomfort. I think about the discomfort of *Time Clock Piece*, or – he did five of these "One Year Performances" – like, once he was tied to the artist Linda Montano with an eight-foot-long piece of rope and they weren't allowed to touch each other the entire time. There was *Cage Piece*, when he made a cell in his studio and entered solitary confinement. He had no entertainment, nothing, not even a pen. All the strain he put himself under makes me think it's possible for me to bear it too. *Rope Piece* makes me think about how we relate to each other now versus the potential community anarchism could engender. I imagine the no-touching rule like bureaucracy intercepting compassion. It makes me think about the desocialization we're experiencing; the fact people who grew up in shit areas are getting priced out of their own networks; the fact that it feels weird to sit so close and make eye contact and pick up your hands and feel them shaking, when that never used to happen before.'

He'd noticed.

'I said that Tehching Hsieh did five "One Year Perform- ances" but I only told you about three of them: another was to not make art for a year, and then there was *Outdoor Piece* in 1981 where he vowed, "I shall not go into a building, subway, train, car, airplane, ship, cave, tent." And d'ya know what, he didn't, but he also sort of did. The New York Police Department arrested him off the street and forced him into a precinct for fifteen hours, which not only challenged the integrity of the performance, but also the integrity of his place in the city, because he was an illegal immigrant from Taiwan at the time – and I fucking hate saying that. *Illegal immi- grant.* That's the state's language, not mine. It's ridiculous that governments across the globe won't grant us the right to free movement. Who are they to decide where we go and what we do? They don't own us. But they say Travellers are trespassing, and the public goes along with it. They make a new "Public Order Bill" that says, yeah, you can protest, but only if you do it in this really polite way, where we reserve the right to decide what qualifies as polite – and the public goes along with it. The constant enforcement of rules is so effective that it's more comfortable to go along with them.'

That's probably why so many people end up spending their free time in their own house – not only because it costs so much to do anything nowadays, but it's also the one place people feel free.

'Yeah, and that's really sad – that such a small space is where you feel the most freedom, when there's a whole world out there that you're not allowed to move through. But the state has to keep us unhappy and it has to keep us tense and separate and tired and preoccupied because if we realized how free we could be without their intervention – well, then that's it, isn't it? They'd be *fucked*. There's so much design getting in the way of this—'

He squeezed my hands again.

'Listen, it made me sad when you said you haven't told anyone about QT. Is that because you don't want to or because you don't have anyone to tell?'

I mean, I had friends back when I was studying.

'That was a long time ago.'

Yeah, but everyone went their separate ways.

'Community-building means closing the points of difference between people. It's going in and cutting the ropes. I suppose it expects a certain amount of honesty, so it depends if you are willing to tell people about QT.'

I dodged the last part and told Mo if he helped me find comedy-sized ribbon-opening scissors, we could use them to find friends *and* launch the new anarchist world.

'You're saying that like it won't actually happen!'

I can't believe you're here in the flesh, never mind this anarchy business.

'Well, it depends how much you want it.'

Anarchy or you?

'Let's not get ahead of ourselves.'

God, the happiness I want seems so simple on paper. I think: if I work hard enough, I can have it. But it never comes.

'Yeah, it's dogshit. The happiness we want is in all the things the government deprives us of. It's what Lauren Berlant writes about in *Cruel Optimism*. Capitalism tells us that there are certain materialistic things we need in order to be happy, but the closer we get to obtaining them, the further we are from happiness. Because no matter how rich you are, someone else is richer. Those pressures function to keep us wanting, and if that's what you base your happiness on, it'll never end, because you'll never just *be*.'

Why can't I just be?

'Because the state structures every little thing about your existence. If you're a bit short on cash this month, you couldn't set up an impromptu food stand at the end of your road, because of "health and safety". You couldn't sell drawings because you'd need a "street trading licence". You couldn't take QT public and sing whatever AI-generated bullshit QT would sing because you'd need a "busking licence". You'd need to author-ize your busking by showing the council your public liability insurance, and throw in a criminal record check if you decide QT should come dressed like a clown. These measurements might seem harmless enough, but they are means of regulating people. They reveal how the state remains in control of the smallest individ-ual citizen's actions, and *that* is politically ideological; the government wants us to know that we are unable to do anything without them being present in that decision.'

I felt something click, and I told Mo I felt sick, but also excited.

'There's a weird sense of freedom when you realize *why* they'd want us to feel so mollycoddled; and realizing it's not your fault.'

My small resistance in QT really did seem futile. I was almost impressed at the government and the billionaires and the art jury. How did they manage to make us believe that *we* had to answer to *them*?

'That's a big question. But think about the way they speak. Look at the language the media uses to report on shit. The migrant "crisis" for example. The climate "disaster". Everything is presented in a way that makes us hopeless and therefore we think we *must* rely on these people who tell us that we are not equipped to run our own lives. The prime minister needs to do that for us. Who is it again? Whichever shitbag of the month we're on.'

But why do we believe them?

'Because they speak to us with absolute certainty, and most forms of abusive political activity require certainty.'

What do you mean by 'certainty'?

'I mean, if we imagine a situation in which we're going to stop people crossing the Channel in small boats – if you're the sort of person, ethically speaking, who wants to prevent that from happening – you need certainty at the level of argument. In this case, it's that there's not an infinite amount of room on the receiving end and, consequently, you can't have an infinite number going inside it, right? A finite set can't have infinite members, and therefore it's OK if three-year-old Syrian refugees drown in the Channel because your argument is unbeatable, yeah? It's *certain*.'

Is this why I'd found so much reassurance in lying?

'But lying isn't a counter to certainty. Lying is why QT makes me uncomfortable. The best counter is to think about overturning the notion of certainty. You can overturn the sensibleness of the idea that a finite set can't have infinite members, and you can do so by aggressively attacking the notion of the "set" and of "finite-ness", so that politicians don't get to make those kinds of arguments. There are counterpoints to say that, yes, there is enough room and also we're not dealing with an infinite number of people. But another way of doing that is to undermine the idea that those sets and *finities* have any relationship with the world, when they don't. Because even if there was such a thing as infinity, it's not practically manageable for us, nor is the notion of a set. These terms are not actually *certain . . .* Are you still with me?'

No.

'Let's imagine that all common-sense ideas that allow us to make unethical actions in the world are vulnerable by attacking their rationality – it's that unmooring that prevents you from doing unethical things in the first place, because there's never a position from which you could say, *OK, I know this to be true, which is why I act the way I act. I know that you can't have an infinite number of things in a finite set, that's why I let men, women and children die in the English Channel.* You can't have that, because you're never in a position to have certainty and therefore to act unethically. Apply that logic to people dying at sea because they left one piece of land and they're not allowed to come on to another piece of land, and you can see how easy it is for the government to let that happen because the stakes aren't high for them. They keep putting up red tape, and they tell us to abide by it, because they *own* certainty. But it's like, if that was your family in the boat, you wouldn't be doing or saying anything of the sort. All that certainty would go right out the window.'

Yeah, it would.

'It's like people saying they're *not* royalists but they love the royal family. How have these people, who you've never met, convinced you to have more sympathy for them while robbing you of your taxes, but the family from Syria who are fleeing war because they'll be killed – and who arrive here with nothing but trauma – how are they your enemy? What number has the state pulled on you to manipulate that outcome?'

I can't believe we were born in a country that hasn't killed its aristocracy yet.

'Don't. I can't believe we were born in a country with an artistocracy as well. One king is bad enough. I thought the Art King was a myth for so long but apparently not.'

I was busy thinking about the finite sets apparent in art: the number of opportunities compared to the number applying to them; the amount of money compared to the amount bidding for a share of it; the size of the spotlight compared to the legion of artists who deserve it.

'The other way to go about overturning this notion of certainty is to do it *with* art. But not the way you've gone about it.'

QT's number-one hater.

'Reporting for duty. How do you feel about surrealism?'

Surrealism was something I had always avoided in the museum because it made me feel iffy, which sounded childish now that I was saying it out loud.

'No, that's good. That's the point. Any cultural object that makes you feel uncomfortable is useful because it prompts you to come to terms with the reason. It gives you an opportunity to realize how little you struggle with everything around it. The wall, the room, the gallery, the city, the *country* . . . Surrealism is about creating a plastic state in which things can start to change.'

Surrealism is *uncertain*, then.

'Yeah. You've accepted everything around the art as being perfectly rational – as being certain. But why is that? Surrealism attacks in general and across the board any sense that you have certainty sufficient that you can do unethical things. André Breton called it when he wrote "it was in the black mirror of anarchism that surrealism first recognized itself".'

Well, shit. I better brush up on my surrealists.

'Start with Alberto Giacometti.'

The Swiss guy who did those crusty, skinny sculptures? Mrs Kelly got us to make those in class, remember?

'Yeah but he has a lot of other stuff. He made this one thing called *No More Play*. It's a marble slab with rounded divots and there are oblongs cut into the centre like small graves for the game's pieces, which are made of wood. It vaguely resembles a board game, but it's not fucking Monopoly. It's a sculpture. You can't even attempt to play it, because a game is a ruleset you can interact with and this one has no rules. You can't win. There are loads of surrealist objects like that. Salvador Dalí's phone with the lobster receiver; Man Ray's iron with nails down the centre – the one that would rip clothes if someone was stupid or sadistic enough to use it. Stuff that was functional except the artist has transformed it into a dud *so* that we consider how rationality informs everyday domesticity, and how much we accept the form and function of irons and phones – small points into the big, mad questions about how and why we are alive.'

When did Man Ray bedazzle an iron?

'I believe it was in 1921.'

When was the board game made?

'1931.'

And last question, for a million pounds, when did Dalí make the lobster phone?

'Pretty sure it was 1938.'

Those are interesting timings.

'Yeah?'

Depressing timings.

'Depressing because three surrealist objects didn't manage to politicize enough people to defeat fascism and stop the Second World War from happening? I didn't say it was *certain* these methods were gonna bring forth anarchy. I'm not a fucking politician.'

Touché.

'And anyway, fascists aren't interested in being attacked. They weren't interested back then, and they aren't right now. We can try our best to live in a world alongside other people who all have their own desires. We can accept that our only obligation is to the people immediately around us, and we can give those people our attention instead of giving that attention to notions that masquerade as truths; and it used to be religious truths, and it would have been a different set of truths before that. But even if we believe those truths are attackable by art – in that it can undermine our relation-ship with certainty, and use uncertainty as a means of attack – the problem still stands: people in power don't engage with the world in the way they'd need to for those kinds of experiences to change their minds about anything. That's another reason why anarchism is so appealing to me, because anarchism is leaderless. You hear art activists talking about *redistributing power*, but I don't like that. Where there is authority, there is abuse of power. *I think everything could be great if only everybody listened to me.* No. Why don't you fuck off and leave the rest of us alone? Someone who decides they're going to be a leader of people – how do they have the audacity to think they know better about someone else's life than the person living it already does?'

I thought of museum directors, zombies, politicians, critics, influencers, QT. I also thought art was attractive enough to make power pay attention to it. Mo shook his head.

'It's not about acknowledging a thing exists. With culture, we're trying to process our ideas about the world through creative interventions. You and me know this, we feel it. But *contemporary* culture –' he pointed at the door back into the art fair – 'has become so good at commodifying art to the point where even the most subtle experience is only there for us to experience it. As in, we don't think it's there for us to be *changed* by it. The moment you stick art in a booth, it's a product to buy. The moment you so much as stick something in a frame, you're in trouble. Everybody knows they can invalidate it the moment they see it, because that's *art* and that's an important thing that must be worth a lot of money, therefore you don't have to think about it too carefully.'

When Mo had mentioned Dalí's lobster, I knew exactly what he was talking about even though I hadn't seen the sculpture in person because it had appeared on so much museum gift-shop merchandise over the years. T-shirts, magnets, stickers, pencil toppers, tote bags. If I saw the actual thing on a plinth, it wouldn't make me question rationality; I would only see it as a gag.

'And therein lies the problem. High culture loves to appropriate counterculture. It's like, for radical artists, two paths lie before them. They either let the establishment drown them in capital, tie them up with terms and conditions. That path means the establishment absorbs the threat completely. Then say there's a queer, feminist, anti-racist group that the establishment doesn't want. They can ignore it or deny it funding. Let it die. Whether it's bloating the radical art, gatekeeping it or freezing it out, all paths lead to the establishment's victory. The poor artist can't win.'

He smiled, and it surprised me, because this wasn't a very happy conversation.

'I reckon this is why I ended up getting into criticism, ya know? Art degrees teach critical thinking, and now all I can do is critique the art industry. This writer gig sent me to Cyprus recently, and while I was there I met phytorio, an association of artists and theorists. They do exhibitions, the usual. But they also act as a lobbying group in the most amazing way. There's legislation in Cyprus that stipulates public buildings must spend one per cent of their budget on public art. But what phytorio have found is that people take that as a suggestion rather than a legal requirement. So, phytorio works with lawyers to light a fire under the people responsible. They get in touch, remind them of the law, offer to support them in selecting work. But if there's no movement, they simply file a lawsuit, and then people put their hands in their pockets. They are playing them at their own game.'

I wish they didn't have to go to all that trouble.

'Me too. Making art is such a lively way to spend a life, and yet, all the structures surrounding art are lifeless. Artists need structural advantages to get in *and* to stay in. It's all about money, and that is gutting because the amount of money somebody owns isn't necessarily up to them.'

All artists must have a knackered art critic trapped inside them. My inner critic is aiming all its vitriol at the funding model, which is supposed to be a great leveller against systemic advantage, something we are supposed to celebrate. But it doesn't work.

'Oh, but it works exactly like they want it to. It stops that pure carefree art-making that artists tend towards. Because in order to bid for money, those carefree tendencies have to be rationalized using very specific language on very elaborate application forms where they're saying, *art has to be rationalized before it is allowed to happen*, because it's safer for them if art is vetted; if every idea has sound logic behind it. But art doesn't have to mean anything. Art doesn't always have to be planned. Why can't stuff just *be* because it *is*.'

195

Like art after anarchism.

'That's what I've been saying!'

It would make so much sense.

'And people think the idea of governance is *sensible*; they think Arts Council England divvying out cultural funding is *sensible*. *People* need to give their heads a wobble, because how sensible is it that we accept a governmental hierarchy of what culture is acceptable and worthy of receiving public funding, and what culture is illegal? A kid who wants to graffiti a wall because they think graffiti is cool and that's how they want to express themselves can't try it without risking a criminal record for vandalism. But the same police don't seriously pursue Banksy for a conviction because he's already been appropriated. His graffiti is *street art*.'

Speaking to you is making me nostalgic for simpler times, but things weren't simple even then.

'Quest, we don't *know* how bad we've got it.'

It feels pretty bad to me.

'I mean, we don't know how bad we've got it *now*. I'm in a studio group back home—'

In Glasgow?

'No, I moved back to Liverpool years ago, and right, I have a desk there and two of the studio members, John and Sheila, were telling me they found an empty space on Renshaw Street – and this is going back twenty years – but the doors were soldered shut. So what did they do? They took an angle grinder to it in the middle of the night. That's metal as fuck. That's where their studios were before they moved into the building we're in now. They had a gallery, they put the electricity on the fiddle. I was asking Sheila about it because I couldn't imagine ever pulling something like that off now. She said, someone would rock up and ask, can I do this performance here? And they didn't have to weigh up the financial risk. *Is it going to work? Isn't it going to work?* It didn't matter. It only mattered that it happened.'

I could have had an exhibition there if I'd been born sooner.

'It *killed* me. She said, *you were left to make what you wanted to make, and have a laugh, and get on with it.* We've properly internalized that funding system with its green lights and its red lights and its fucking strobe lights, and now we all wait for permission to do some-thing instead of making what we want, and having a laugh, and getting on with it.'

Yeah but we *have* to wait for funding to give us the go-ahead because no one has disposable income for studio space and studio time – the stuff that leads to an exhibition. I think we were born at the wrong time.

'It's funny that, isn't it? We grow up thinking that the time we're living in is the most progressive. But there is no such thing as linear progress. There have been times in history when we've been freer than we are right now. It's Roe v. Wade. It's Francis Fukuyama believing the liberal project will end with a free society. It's bollocks. The world that we live in is failing, and it will fail, and it'll be gone. The anarchism that I want to happen is basically inevitable, but the sad thing is it won't happen for us. It may only happen for a very dwindled subset of humanity, even though it *could* happen sooner if there were enough of us willing to bring on a revolution.'

That's a big word.

'I dunno if it is. It's just bringing the end times forward so that we can have that life now. But it doesn't matter. Eventually, all of this stuff will disappear anyway, because they'll fuck the world up to such an extent that everything will be impossible – and climate collapse is upon us and every masterpiece will end up in the sea, and all we'll have left is people who have to rely on each other in order to survive, and then there *will* be an importance to your individual being in the world because there will be so few of us that we'll go back to being essential to each other.'

Sounds like a good time.

'Yeah. When you're home next, we should work on some of this stuff together.'

We should.

'Do you want to collaborate with me?'

I do.

'If we do it together, it might be easier for you to let QT go.'

The gallerist came trotting outside.

'April, the buyer who put *Green Piece V* on hold wants to go through with the sale. I need you to come inside and sign off on it. Now.'

I stood up without any hesitation because standing up meant accepting money, and money meant comfort, and Mo would understand because the utopia he was pitching me wasn't real, not yet anyway. The gallerist looked like she was going to piss herself with excitement.

'She's. A buyer. For the King.'

I turned to wave, but Mo was already gone.

Certainty

In 2014, two unarmed teenagers, Mohammad Abu Daher and Nadeem Nawara, were shot and killed by an Israeli border guard in the occupied West Bank. Israel claimed they used legal rubber-coated steel bullets to deter the Palestinian children, but audio analysis by the artist Lawrence Abu Hamdan revealed it was in fact the illegal use of live ammunition that killed Mohammad and Nadeem. The artist did his analysis on the invitation of Forensic Architecture, who investigate human rights violations on behalf of 'communities and individuals affected by conflict, police brutality, border regimes and environmental violence'.[34] Abu Hamdan made visual representations of the sound frequencies of the ballistics, and his report was used in court by the prosecution. Forensic Architecture rebukes the certainty of the state with the certainty of evidence.

In 1977, the Puerto Rican artist Papo Colo strapped fifty-one planks of wood to his body with ropes around his arms, waist and feet, and ran down the West Side

---

34. From Forensic Architecture's website, accessed November 2023: https://forensic-architecture.org/about/agency

Highway in Manhattan until he collapsed out of exhaustion. The performance took place a year after the US Congress denied Puerto Rico's bid for statehood, a change which would have seen an increase in federal funding and given Puerto Ricans the right to vote in US elections. Appearing like a marionette that had escaped his puppeteer's control, Colo performed the weight of bureaucratic certainty and, with the cumbersome wood and rope dragging on the street behind him, our failure to completely outrun it.

Before Sonia Boyce's retrospective opened at Manchester Art Gallery in 2018, the artist arranged for the temporary removal of J. W. Waterhouse's 1896 painting *Hylas and the Nymphs*. In doing so, Boyce invited staff and visitors to consider which works deserved wallspace and which works should be put into storage. The culture we are exposed to helps us to create meaning. The culture we aren't ever shown limits how far that meaning can go. Curators hold an immense power in making such decisions for us. When somebody is shown a breadth of cultural objects from across time, space and people, if that person is more familiar with the creation of meaning, they are more able to see the creation of *certainty* for what it is, a *creation.*

In 1982, Agnes Denes planted and harvested a two-acre wheatfield on a landfill in Manhattan. The sight of natural bright-gold wheat growing out of the ground against the unnatural grey of built-up New York created a surreal statement, in what looked almost like a collaged scene, or a portal that could return Earth back to nature. Denes used surrealism to get us to question our use of land and our blatant interruption of natural ecologies. In the artwork's contentious placement, just two blocks away from Wall Street, she also invited us to think about food production, hunger, waste, trade, pollution and the many systems of inequality we believe to be permanent and *certain*.

In 2008, a busy audience at Tate Modern were confronted by police officers mounted on horses using crowd control manoeuvres against them. Visitors were not told beforehand that it had anything to do with art. That way, they could experience the full force of police controlling their movement around the gallery; and they would feel the imposition as a vulnerable individual, and not as a safe audience spectating a performance. It was only later revealed as a piece by Cuban artist Tania Bruguera. Bruguera used the simulation to demonstrate how mounted police express certainty using intimidation, and how quick the audience was to accept that expression; even when they were inside a so-called *public* institution dedicated to art.

Side Quest #1: The Jupiter Residency

CONFIDENTIAL

THE JUPITER RESIDENCY MISSION REPORT AB-1

Composite air-to-ground voice transcription during orbit. Voice fair to good;[35] bad intermittent static. Communications derived from ground station voice-recording tapes using WhatsApp software.

Prepared by: Quest Talukdar
Mission objective: Cast radio signal. Wait for extraterrestrial response. Build connection.

January

AB: Hi, I'm sorry for the voice transmission. I hope it's OK. It's a lot easier to speak than it is to type. If I look at screens for too long, my eyes feel like shit. If I hold my phone for too long, my hands can't take it. Hello, hi, how's it going? My name is Amelia. I'm glad you

---

35. NASA report, *Apollo 17 Command Module Onboard Voice Transcription*, 1973.

messaged, actually. I also don't speak to other artists enough. What do you make? OK. Out. [END OF TAPE]

February

AB: You want me to go first? Roger that. Except, I don't know what to send you pictures of because I haven't been in an exhibition for years and I don't relate much to the art I was making before I left the planet . . . That sounds cryptic. I should probably give you the Previously On. It was during install when I woke up with the flu. I couldn't get out of bed, but the technicians knew where everything was due to go so they hung my pieces for me. I actually missed my own PV, and I was gutted, because I'd only done exhibitions in artist-led spaces up until that point, and this was a classy mid-tier space. I'd told everyone I'd be OK but maybe I jinxed it. I didn't know it back then, but I'd been flung into perpetual motion, away from the people who were sending pictures from the opening when I couldn't even look at my phone. I was in a bad way. I was waking up feeling like I hadn't slept. Eventually, I crawled to the window and found the whole world upside down.

I was working in a museum café at the time. This shit zero-hour thing that meant no sick pay. At the end of the second week, the manager kept texting me, like: *hello, you should be back in work by now.* I should have been. But tell me how I'm gonna stand behind the counter all day if I nearly fainted waiting for my toast to pop. I couldn't send her a picture of the pain inside my legs as proof. I saw a doctor in week 3, assuming the conversation would play out in good faith once I described how bad I was feeling.

They weren't convinced. It's weird to use that word in particular, but in the first year of sickness, I was having to make the case *for* myself *to* myself every day because I also couldn't believe it. I'd have a moment of okayness and think wow, I was lying to everyone this entire time – and then I'd wash the dishes and have to stop halfway through to lie down for hours. It was messing with my head. But you cannot scream in space. Or you can, but no one will hear you.

Needless to say, I wasn't thinking about art or exhibition culture by that point. It wasn't thinking about me. I moved home. I was living life under an eye mask because perception was too exhausting. My mum drove to the gallery to pick up my work months after the fact, and half of it was missing. The half that wasn't missing was dented. She said she wasn't going to tell me but she needed to explain the damage. I didn't even have the energy to be upset; I wanted the *doctor* to explain the damage. Did I have myalgic encephalomyelitis?[36] Postural orthostatic tachycardia syndrome?[37] All of the above? When you are sick for a very long time, everyone loses interest, even though you

36. ME, also known as chronic fatigue syndrome, affects energy, cognition, sleep and pain.

37. POTS is a blood disorder and heart condition caused by problems with the body's nervous system. Gabrielle de la Puente has it. See her game *People of the Salt*, published on Downpour, 2023.

feel eternally bad, ischaemic,[38] in orbit, far away in a dysautonomic land.[39]

I don't know who I am any more. I'm an enigma, an alien, an Amelia. A post-viral version of myself. An operating system downgrade. It's hard to breathe now. The gravity is stronger where I stand. I'm in a different time zone, and my blood vessels can't handle the summers. I know you only asked to see the art I make but I'm still working through what it means to make art from a recently disabled body. I used to be a person who carried business cards on them at all times but I don't care about that stuff any more. You'll have to go first. You tell me what you make. Over. [END OF TAPE]

April

AB: Copy. Hello, earthling. Reading you loud and clear. See, it's not just me being coy. But I don't get it. Why won't you send me pictures of *your* work? What's your excuse? And what did you say at the end? You wanted to know if I thought business cards were worth it. Er, I mean, they're a bit old school but it's one way of sticking in someone's head: getting nice and withered in their wallet between various fading receipts. People always get too many of

38. Ischaemia means reduced blood flow to a part of the body, resulting in pain and an increased risk of heart attack and stroke.

39. Dysautonomia refers to problems with the body's autonomic nervous system.

them printed. But I'm probably the worst person to ask because I don't actually see anyone.

It's like – you also asked if I still made art, and if I did, was it harder now. (I wonder if you are scared of this happening to you. I think everybody should be afraid of losing their freedom.) There was definitely a stage early on when I was in survival mode and I wasn't thinking about the survival of my 'art career'. But I never let art go, even when things were at their worst – on the bad days, it still keeps me company. I might not be physically upright at an easel, but that doesn't mean I stop thinking about art. I don't think I *can* stop. Art is the thing at the centre of it all. The galleries, curators, and this busy sky of satellites wouldn't be here without the sun holding everything together. I know in myself that when I'm flat out, I still *feel* its pull. Art is the molten core. I live with art in mind, because art is how I interact with the world – it's my default, not just how I approach an image.

When I'm stuck in bed, I don't stop being an artist. Look at Liz Crow – she did that piece where she landed her bed in the gallery for forty-eight hours. She was sick in public. She *couldn't* call in sick! Art is the act of creating a form in which you're asking people to bear witness to you. That's what she did so well, but I don't think I could have appreciated that *before* I got sick. I used to see art so literally. Art was a business; the artist was the supplier; and an artwork was the product. I thought that art meant making something appear out of thin air that hadn't been there before. But that is so limiting. Art is not a solid. It's not even a liquid. It goes beyond materials. It's *inside*. If my surroundings change, if my body changes, that's fine because art is within me.

I mean . . . art is my eyes oscillating between the four corners of the ceiling when my muscles feel like bruised metal, and I'm looking at those four corners in a pattern only I know. Or I don't realize I'm making something, and I mark it in my mind as art like an afterthought; as though I've given a moment in time parentheses. There doesn't have to be an audience for those acts. There doesn't have to be an exhibition. In fact, I think it's better if there isn't one; it's more sincere. The type of work I make isn't very marketable anyway. My marginalization is in direct conflict with marketability. No collector wants to buy a piece of work to do good by a disabled person. They want art that will increase in value, and for that, I'm dirt.

But I'm not thinking about any of that Earth-shit when other sick people give me their art. I'm just thinking, great, now I don't need to figure out how to express this particular facet of disability. I feel more understood in art than I do at the doctor's surgery. That's what I thought when I found RA Walden's x̌ây ithřa. The artist collaborated with the linguist Margaret Ransdell-Green to create a language that pinches sick thoughts into new words. Back when I was running around London pulsing from show to show, I used to be *dŷathatŷatŷe*, 'someone who is so attached to their own health and strength that when sickness comes it will be a great shock'. I went through *ówasheyalax̌atsŷiha* when I closed the curtains for two

208

years. That's 'the feeling of loss when you first realize that you are not in control of your body'. Now I am left with unending *ówashehalaẍadŷiwa*, which is 'the loss of realizing someone you love will never understand what it's like for you to move through the world'.

RA Walden's word for body, *Yala*, is the same word they use for home and planet Earth. It's also the only word that is capitalized in the whole of ẍây ithřa, and it means that when you're connecting with the language, you're also connecting with the Earth. It absolutely fucks me up every time I think about it, because I can feel in my belly that the artist is speaking to me. Maybe not you. Just me. It made me laugh when you asked if it's harder to make art now, because of course it is. But I used to think sickness meant a person must be vomiting or bleeding or whatever. If a sick person was making art, they can't really be sick. I didn't understand that the sick person might only be able to work a lump of clay for an hour because they'd spent a day resting beforehand and they'd cleared their schedule so that they could recover from the exertion. I have the kind of illness that I can speed away from like a getaway car down a motorway until the inevitable crash.

That defiance is helped by the rails I've got installed everywhere, the walking stick, the mobility scooter, the compression clothing, the medication. My energy is up and down, always fluctuating, and I have learnt to use those waves as jumping-off points. I like it when I get so absorbed in making a piece of art that I forget how much pain I'm in because I'm enjoying it *that* much – and in the course of making, I'll come to a turn, or trip up, or find there's a material I need that I don't have, and I'll come out of the reverie and – shit, *now the pain is hot and loud inside me.*

That's a quirk of chronic illness that's hard to discuss with someone who hasn't gone through it. The quote-unquote *bad behaviour*. For example, I can't lift much weight so I *should* make light, ephemeral artworks, and I shouldn't make a mess when I can't bend down to tidy up after myself; but that spurs me on to make incredibly heavy pieces that take ten people to move. I let the mess be a mess. For all I know, you might be listening and thinking, *if it hurts that much, then stop. Art is not worth putting yourself through this discomfort.* It might even look like self-harm from the outside, but my *self* is always in harm's way. If I have to do life on hard mode, how do I need to prepare so that I can keep beating sickness in these small ways?

One of my sick friends hides from his carer and his partner to draw flash tattoos on the loo, and he *has* to hide because the carer-partner duo will team up and tell him rest is best. But sometimes making art is more important than rest. It definitely is if my mate is hiding in the bathroom to get alone time with it. When Virginia Woolf said, 'A Room of One's Own', maybe she meant the loo. Other sick friends sidestep the bathroom completely and they let themselves get disgusting. They don't wash because washing uses energy that could be better spent on art-making. The dishes pile up and the bins don't get taken out. But some of us only get to do one thing a day – if that – and I'm obviously going to choose the thing that makes me the happiest. The thing that makes me feel most like myself. I'm not thinking about the volume of art I make, or the consistency, or the mastery. All I'm thinking is: how can I get this thing where I want it to be? And anyway, this is why dry shampoo exists!

OK, if that is enough to scare you off, I'll say my goodbyes across the universe. If not, tell me why *you* don't want to send me pictures of *your* work. Tell me if art is how you interact with the world. How's it going down on *Yala*? I reckon I could send you pictures of the new stuff I've been making, if you want? Over and out. [END OF TAPE]

Early September:
AB: Sorry for the radio silence. It was summer so I had to die. Your message said that you'd tried to find photos of my art by searching my name, but I deleted my website and social media. I don't want to show my art to someone who isn't disabled. Not everything I make is about disability but these recent pieces have disability as the subject. I've been obsessed with the idea that different artworks address different parts of the body. A small, head-sized painting hung at eye level might want to address the head; a human-sized marble statue might want to address the whole body; something slight on a low plinth might speak to the hands by our sides as we approach it; a tapestry across a wall addresses multiple people at once. I've been considering what *category of* audience I want to address with my work, and it's making me want to be even more

careful with it. So yeah, I'm sorry, but I can't send these pictures to you. I hope that's OK. You still didn't send me yours to be fair. Out. [END OF TAPE]

Late September
AB: Yeah, I'm happy to explain. I am so put off by how art institutions pathologize disability – both museums and funding bodies – as if I don't get enough of that from medical institutions. I don't want to feel abnormal going into a meeting with a curator, and I don't want to feel abnormal going into a meeting with a doctor either. Other artists are better at navigating that. I've known sick people who have come to the end of what the NHS can offer them, and they've actually turned to art for more active support. I know one writer, Abi Palmer, who wrote a funding application for research and development that took place in a thermal spa that not only rehabilitated her body to give her the capacity to write, but also provided the subject matter for her book, *Sanatorium*. The Arts Council covered the writer's medical bills. I think: wow, that's genius. People shouldn't have to write arduous funding applications to ease their pain, even temporarily. But these are the things we have to do.

It's wild that funding can mean an artist's needs are accommodated for the first time ever, when access to arts funding is as much of a gamble as hoping to get a well-read, not completely burnt-out doctor when you call your GP. It's like, you win your Paul Hamlyn Foundation grant or you don't, and that determines whether or not you get to be well that year. You get your commission or you don't, and that determines whether or not you get to be well that month. I talk a lot with other disabled artists about not going for the £250 and £500 microgrants because given the amount of work it takes to apply for them, along with the energy to create the art, and play by the funder's rules for actually getting paid, it's never equitable. But money is the closest thing we've got to a panacea, so how can we ever say no?

And so we say yes, we will work with the institutions, and the institutions want us because they know we are disabled, and that's not curation, that's ethnography, so it's no wonder the curator goes on to place little value on our time. They won't respect lateness or cancellations. They'll be sending emails saying 'we need that by tomorrow' but what do they want us to do if we aren't seeing our support worker until Friday – or the sick person who has no help is on week two of a migraine? Healthy people want everything right this instant, but my time is worth more than a micro-grant promises. It *has* to be. It would be more true of my body, and it would be much easier to work with me, if the process of working together acknowledged the inevitable interruptions and mistakes. What about the aftercare, as well? What if there was money set aside to cover how exhausted I am going to feel once the work is done? It's easier if I just . . . don't.

There was a time when I was even happy to be used as a tick box for funding if a curator was frank with me because I know how this stuff works, but no one was ever frank because they knew there was something wrong with the system. If an opportunity is really gauche and offensive, I know artists who will double their fee in order to swallow it. I get it, but I wish I didn't. I don't even want to be contacted by these people any more, that's why I took my website down. I don't want to be questioning whether or not I am ticking a box for them, or if they are genuinely interested in my ideas. Sometimes it's blatant. Just artists grouped badly together around the theme of having a sick body. That's a shit theme for an exhibition. Everyone's having a terrible time, come see art about it! And this is always coming from galleries that stop making events accessible as soon as the *disabled* one's over. That is why I deleted my website, so the galleries can no longer find me. That is why I'm 645.85 million kilometres away.

To go back to my original point, I don't want to show you what I've been working on because while I have a huge desire to make art, I have this growing repulsion towards exhibition and display. I can feel myself starting to have a *bigger* desire for secrecy, and I guess that is because it does not open me up to disrespect. If I were to put my website back up and a gallery got hold of them, the press release would say something like: *in her latest series, Amelia Bridge paints a prone clothed figure in holiday resorts around the world. Referencing the disability that inhibits her from travelling to these exotic places, the images are an exercise in imagination, invisible borders, and . . .* bravery? I don't know. They love saying shit like that. You'd then get an audience who are, by default of them even being in the gallery, the wrong audience to bear witness to the paintings. It really stings to think about all the art that is produced with public funding, yet so much of the public never even get to see it, because they're sick and unpublicized.

No, if I sent photos of the paintings to you, you'd see destinations of places that don't exist for me any more. I don't have the energy to get there, and even if I did, I'd be like the girl in the paintings: prone and half-clothed at the all-inclusive buffet. I'm joking but that's a case of the difference between us, and I don't *want* the paintings to be about the difference between us. I want them to be about dreaming of going somewhere but not being able to, and for the point of the painting to end there. They should only be seen by people who know where that ending is, not by people who can step over the ending and carry on down the lazy river.

Healthy audiences tend to pity disabled characters in art, even if the artist didn't mean for that to happen, *or* the audience. I really don't want pity. I also don't want to have to declare I don't want pity. I want the opposite of all of that! I want 'access intimacy', the phrase Mia Mingus coined – which has its own word in ẍây ithřa, by the way – I told you about that, didn't I? It's *méalâřinŷâ*. Access intimacy is the ease I feel when I speak to other disabled people and we don't *need* to explain ourselves. It's the unmasking we feel when we visit each other's planets, and we're no longer trying to keep up with anyone else. If art has to have an audience, it would feel *good* to offer something exclusive to people excluded from so much.

And why shouldn't I make up my own rules? Sick artists have done an excellent job of working with and against the rules of art institutions. They have to – they can't do anything else. If they don't make art their job, they can't do it at all, because they don't have capacity for more; and most jobs don't accommodate for the waves, so *artist* becomes the only role that fits. I left that behind when I left Earth. I look at these paintings and I know they should not end up in galleries. They'd do better on bedroom walls or hung over couches. Pinned to the ceiling so there's something to stare at other than concentric Artex lines. They should be in hospitals, doctors' waiting rooms; they should be sent in the post to continue slow friendships with the sick people I know across the solar system. Return address: The Jupiter Residency. A sanctuary I've made for myself where there is no such thing as business cards and funding applications, and no curators selling snake oil. No art market, no critics, no meetings, no calendars – no time at all. Only me floating in crip time through a bunch of swirling gases, milk and taupe. They brush against the windows of my spaceship and bubble in the heavy air that I might always struggle to breathe. [END OF TRANSCRIPT]

No more transmissions received.

Side Quest #2: Art Hospital

'. . . and the doctors in the Art Hospital told me not to use my hands because how will they ever heal if I'm tip-tap-typing, but I'm on pain meds so I can't feel them anyway. I'm also bored in the ward and none of you fuckers have been to visit yet. One of the nurses told me he saw the article on the *Art Newspaper*, and everyone is cancelling Jake, and I knew I had to go live. I've never been live before, but I've watched enough YouTube to pull off a story time. I'm gonna call it BURNT MY HANDS OFF or TELLING THE TRUTH ABOUT MY BOSS. More people are tuning in. Oh, there's a comment. Quest! I haven't seen you since we were yay high. God, I wouldn't be here now if my Masi hadn't taken me to the baby group in the museum. How are they treating me? I mean, it's busy here today. Gastro-enterology is full of painters who accidentally took a swig of turps instead of the cup of tea next to it. There were rows of miserable-looking people in the ENT waiting room: sound artists who don't know how to turn the volume down; singers with nodes; ceramicists who forgot to turn on the extractor. When I came through A&E, there were tourists who'd tripped over the crack

Doris Salcedo built into the floor of Tate Modern to express grand ideas about borders and immigration. I heard the head of security huffing and puffing and explaining that "physical protection measures which would normally be applied to a gap of this nature are not deemed appropriate due to its artistic nature", and for once, I agree with the Tate! The nation state is a racist construct and visitors *should* twist their ankle. It's only fair. At least they get to leave this place. Do you remember when Jeanne-Claude and Christo installed those parasols in Ibaraki and California and one of them crushed a woman in the US, and another one electro-cuted a Japanese worker during deinstall? Two deaths! Artists are a liability. *Why* we do these things, I'll never know. When I was doing a Foundation Diploma, the tutors scared us into doing risk assessments by telling us about a foundation student who had collected bird poo off her bedroom window to make jewellery with. She ended up in the Art Hospital but I'm sure artists will continue to use biological matter and massive umbrel-las. The doctors can tell us scalpels are for surgeons not collage, but try telling Mary Evans that. Try telling John Stezaker. We won't listen! Case in point: my hands. Can you see them? Red raw. God, where do I begin?

'Jake asked me to prep aluminium for the next installa-tion. I've done it loads of times. I enjoy it, and that's part of the problem. The surface of the metal is greasy so you need to sand it to change its porosity. Once the metal's sanded, you send a current through it to impregnate a powder coating. That way, you can change the colour and it won't chip. It can withstand kids, birds, art critics. I guess I sanded too many too quickly, and we had a deadline. His sculptures are so popular at the moment. The only way he can keep up with the demand is to employ a team of assistants to fabricate the work for him. I was there really late. We all were. And the machine vibrates *a lot*. Plus, I wasn't wearing gloves because I wanted to be really precise with my handiwork and that's on me. No, like, it actually is. I *was* supposed to be wearing protective gear, but when you've been doing something long enough – and Jake never wears them – I start big and I apply a lot of pressure, and then the process gets more delicate. That's partly because Jake doesn't want me to leave any evidence of sanding on the surface. I had to get it done in time, because us getting it done in time means the work can go to art fairs and sculpture parks, and get sold, and that money keeps the studio in business and us in work and – the bar slipped and I went to grab it and my hands were on the sander and next thing I know, I'm here speaking to you.

'The doctor who saw me first was saying, "I bet you hope this heals fast, don't you? You're gonna wanna go back and finish the job?" He's so used to artists doing what they want. But I've been that man's assistant for over five years and now I'm in the burns unit. I've assisted artists ever since I wanted to be an artist myself, because I thought that was a solid way to learn how artists work; to hear the language they use, watch their thought processes in action. I never went to university, but I imagine my workplace must be similar – the studio is a place where people *speak of art*, there's hands-on learning, and everyone in the room can share in art together. But to start with, I was only ever helping artists with events: serving drinks at openings, making deliveries, leafleting, stewarding during public perform-ances, which is fine but I didn't learn anything new, although I did appreciate getting to wear a hi-vis vest.

'And then I got the job working for Jake, and it was totally different and empowering because he had us making pieces from beginning to end. I *know* so much now. I can sew. I've got pretty good at spray painting. The other assistants taught me how to use the heavy machinery he's got for wood and metal. I know how to use a camera now, how to retouch photos, how to get them ready for printing; how to shoot films, how to use editing software. I did time in the office upstairs checking inventory, ordering materials, coordinating with galleries and creating a proper filing system for the archives. The admin side of things was interesting, even if it taught me I didn't want to do it – I did just want to make stuff. There was a point when the office work got too much for me, and I had to say to Jake that I couldn't be responsible for someone else's life. To his credit, I was back in the workshop the next day.

'Listen, I can see your comments. I'm trying to give you the full picture, because it's not like all bosses are evil and all workers are saints. Sure, other people have a really hard time working for artists, having to deal with certain personalities and all their anxieties, which they hope will become your anxieties too. I know it wasn't *my artwork*, but I cared about it. I liked being part of the team. I liked that, instead of paying a university, I was the one getting paid to learn, make and socialize. I liked that we were all working in service of art and not some horrible corporation.

'I just . . . got into this thinking I would be having my own exhibitions by now. And instead, I've been doing a degree in the subject of Jake's creativity. I think the painkillers are starting to wear off. I keep thinking about Divine in the film *Female Trouble*, the one by John Waters. When she rubs herself down with dead fish and pretends to suck off a gun, and the audience eats up her every word, even when she gives a speech claiming this long list of notorious crimes. They're so mesmerized by her look and her constitution and the power in her voice that when she point-blank asks, "Who wants to be famous? Who wants to die for art?" a man springs up into the air and she shoots him dead, and everyone freaks out because they thought she was only putting on a performance. I got way too close to the stage.

'And I know why. The job wasn't only *taking* from me, it was giving something back – validation, community. Artistic communities are built by matchmakers. At openings, Jake would say, *Sangita has a practice.* He made it clear I was an artist in my own right, and the studio was not only aimed at his work but also at everybody else's. We'd share what we were working on, and conversations would turn into spontaneous crits. Jake liked that because it meant new concerns were always coming to him through us and that thing happened – conversations around the work inevitably informed the work. Sometimes, I think the only possible way for me to move forward with my thinking, the only way for me to have new ideas even, is to talk shit with other artists and see what comes out. Jake got to enjoy that atmosphere for the four days a week we were in the studio, which is good for him; he set Fridays aside so he could work on his own and process what had been said.

'He was so generous with his materials. I started using metal in my own practice because he let me have his scraps. After sanding his stuff to perfection, I wanted to make a point of leaving the sanding marks apparent in *my* work. I left a pattern on the surface. I remember showing him what I'd made and we got into a really good discussion about production and quality. I was always trying to skip to the final outcome to get to the good part, but what if the process was the good part? I started thinking about how big artists have teams supporting them, and how I was part of that process now. Jake's sculptures tried to hide the studio. His pieces *became* art through precision. Jake needed the studio's help to maintain that standard. I do wonder what art I would be making if I had the same resources. Like, what art could I *only* make with the backing of an entire team? I don't have answers. I imagine those kinds of ideas only come once you have the means – but it also might be a mistake to hire others.

'I went to a Canaletto exhibition once, the Venetian painter, and there was a noticeable difference in the look and feel of his work before and after he started using assistants. There was a new mechanical deadness to the paintings because the figures were painted in the same repetitive way. Dab, dab, dab, coat, coat, coat, hat, hat, hat, stick, stick, stick. They were a copy–paste job. The art stopped feeling instinctive. Even back then, I preferred being able to see the artist's touch, and this was long before I joined Jake's studio. I actually like it when an artist does something wrong in the right way. That's so human – when it feels like a save, like the success of the piece is teetering on the edge of some-thing and thankfully it never quite fell. I don't think you can engineer the same drama if there are assistants ready to swoop in and save the work – like I'm sure someone's doing now while I sit in hospital waiting for my epidermis to return from the war.

'Sorry, if it wasn't already clear: this is my . . . *resignation livestream*. I don't blame the man. He wasn't holding my hands down. It's more a moment to consider the environment that successful, busy, ambitious artists have to create in order to keep up with their own careers. It can be enjoyable to help these artists achieve something they couldn't pull off alone, but I don't think I'm willing to do it any more. Years ago, I told my sister about this job and she couldn't get her head around it. She kept saying I was being exploited because I was making someone else's art, but as I said, I didn't care about credit. They weren't my ideas or my aesthetics. Jake always made the first version and he taught us how to emulate him. I was, and always have been, fine with that. They're not to my taste. But I know credit is contentious. I've always really liked Christian Marclay's twenty-four-hour-long film, *The Clock*. It montages thousands of scenes from TV and film that show the time, and the edit orders the clips so that the artwork can actually function as a clock. I read loads of interviews he did about the piece, and he'd sometimes mention this team of six mysterious assistants. I wonder who they were. Because if I got people to spend years scouring centuries of footage to make my special clock film that everyone raves about – that people queue up for, and come to museums all the way through the night to get the full experience – I don't think I'd be able to help myself saying their names. It's funny that when you get to the end of a normal film, there's like ten minutes of credits, but *The Clock* doesn't have *any* because otherwise it would no longer be in sync.

'I dunno! I don't love the strict individualization of that way of working. I don't love the fact your name is so significant in this industry that it has to be heard on its own. It's not that I think people shouldn't work together, it's more that the literal production of art is kept in the shadows and that is disingenuous. It upholds the notion that the artist did the thing on their own so the artwork belongs only to them; they are the singular genius in a world where ideas are more valuable than the labour it takes to bring those ideas to life. That makes me feel woozy, and I'm already pretty nauseous. I think what I *really* want is full-on *Lord of the Rings* credits at the end of an artwork. I want a book-style appendix with references, citations, *acknowledgements.* Even if the assistant doesn't wanna name themselves – because I get it – I want to know how many hours of assistance the artwork benefited from. I want to see the email chains. The funder, the budget, the project timeline. I want to know what the curator's input was. The commissioner's. I want to know the health status of the artist. The wealth status too. I want to know what actually had to happen for the art to come about because I want to know how artists make *any* of this happen. It's a fucking mystery how anyone gets into a position where they can make art, let alone hire other people to make it for them. The ones who pull it off should share those secrets at every opportunity so the rest of us don't feel like shit.

'And if the artist won't tell us who helps them – if their secret team is kept in the shadows – how can we know those people are safe? Stop typing "Injury Lawyers 4U" in the comments! I'm not going to sue him. It's not like I would know how to run a studio perfectly if I was in his position. Artists know how to make art, they don't automatically know how to run businesses. So much of being an artist is figuring it out as you go along and, today, we all did a bit more of that. Everyone in this hospital did. No actually, stop commenting. I *am* in a union – I'm in two. I'm in Artists' Union England *and* I'm in BECTU.[40] I'm not suing anyone. I've literally done Jake's books, I know he doesn't have the money to be sued. He is covering my sick pay while I wait till the skin grows back, and then I'm going to figure out a way to recover my own identity. OK? You'd better come and visit me. *Excuse me. Can you please turn this off for me? I can't use my hands.*'

---

40. Broadcasting, Entertainment, Communications and Theatre Union, a trade union for people in the creative and media industries.

Inquest

In 1997, the Belgian artist Francis Alÿs pushed a slab of ice through the streets of Mexico City. Starting out the size of a suitcase, eventually becoming small enough for Alÿs to kick it along the floor, the ice lasted ninety minutes before it completely melted. The artist later shared a video of the performance with an opening title that read, 'sometimes making something leads to nothing', but it didn't quite lead to *nothing.* The artist had a film, and the people of Mexico City had a new story about a strange man pushing a block of ice with one hand and smoking a cigarette with the other.

In 2014, the Cuban artist Carlos Martiel had nylon strands stitched through his torso and tied to the walls of a gallery. Martiel had to stay as still as possible so as not to tug on his skin and cause pain, but there were involuntary movements picked up by silver bells that hung from each taut string. The sound of the bells created a harmony at odds with the torturous scene; the accidental ringing of the bells exposed the liveliness of what it means to exist in a human body. Artists become attached to institutions and leaving them behind can cause real pain.

In 2010, the Dutch artist Aernout Mik invited a large group to gather in Warsaw's largest ex-Soviet building, the Palace for Culture and Science, for an unspecified political meeting. Performers moved between rows of red velvet seats, waved pink flags and papers, took votes, distributed leaflets and delivered impassioned speeches. It is not clear what any of these people were supposed to stand for because Mik's film of the meeting has no audio. The artwork is a mute performance of politics. It is also a blank slate the audience might project on to if they have something they care about as much as the people on the screen.

In 1970, the artist Lee Lozano began leaving the art world. First, she boycotted galleries and dealers. Then, she cut holes in her paintings. She struggled to pay rent on her studio and eventually had to leave it. Lozano marked her exit by calling it her *Dropout Piece*, writing, 'I will be human first, artist second. I will not seek fame, publicity, or suckcess.' She stopped speaking to her collaborators and left New York for Dallas, while we are left to wonder if a piece about no longer making art is in fact a piece, or if the absence of the artist means an absence of art; a hole in a painting that we sink our questions into.

Nineteenth-Century French Painter Gustave Courbet

You didn't need to make good art to be a successful artist; it was the business of art you had to be good at. The only issue was, I didn't *want* to be a business-woman. I wanted to be an artist, and after the art fair, I felt like I was finally getting there, or QT was anyway. We had an invitation from the Art King to attend his annual summer fundraiser, and I *had* to go. It was held on *palace grounds*. The Uber driver that came to fetch me was wearing a frock coat, and smoking a pipe, and I was so excited I didn't realize he could barely drive.

'What is this contraption? Is this *motorized*? *Mon Dieu*. *Where* are we headed?'

I reminded the man that the Art King had summoned me and he somehow knew to slam on the brakes.

'The King? We already fought and died for the universal republic.'

I checked the app to see if the drop-off time was still looking polite, and I had to squint at the driver's details because his profile said that his name was Monsieur Gustave Courbet.

'Mademoiselle, I believe I have been kidnapped by the writers of this book to scare you shitless.'

Painter. Ghost. First-time driver. I was definitely afraid. But I told Monsieur Courbet not to worry. It would be great if we lived in a world without governments and institutions and powerful people, but we don't, they exist, and *I* was hoodwinking the lot of them. With my art, I was inside the tent pissing out.

'Pah! With art? You are inside the tent pissing all over yourself. Back in my day, we pulled down statues of tyrants. Before we had the guillotine the revolutionaries before us would string people up on lampposts. There was even a slogan: "À la lanterne!" Why are the youth so shy about a little revolution? You have everything to gain.'

He started driving, and I nervously laughed the way you do when a taxi driver says something conspiratorial and you are his captive audience.

'In 1870, the French Imperial government provoked a foolish war with our neighbours. The Prussians forced the French generals to retreat, captured our Emperor, Napoleon III, and besieged Paris. Useless politicians, useless generals. *Plus ça change*. The people of Paris were left to starve by their rulers, but we did not take it lying down. We built barricades along the grand boulevards and fought off the soldiers – French and Prussian alike. Where once before they had cried *Vive la révolution,* we cried *Vive la Commune!* For two months, one week and three days, the people of Paris governed themselves in the Paris Commune. We were called Communards. We hung red flags and we abolished the death penalty, military conscription and child labour. We mandated the separation of church and state, returned rent payments to tenants and started paying out our own pension.'

Why are you telling me this?

'Because in the Commune, we formed the Federation of Artists, which included everyone who exhibited in Paris –' he looked at me in the rear-view mirror – 'including women. Artists voted to elect a committee and, for my part, I was elected as delegate for the 6th arrondissement. The committee was responsible for organizing exhibitions and conferences, preserving monuments and museums, and supervising education at the art school. Arts education was undertaken at the expense of the Commune, *rather* than the individual.'

I wonder if I could go back in time with Courbet for some time-travel pre-Brexit Erasmus.

'Our aim was to make art a right that all the people of Paris were entitled to. It had been controlled by the elite for far too long. That's not how art should be. Artists must be equals amongst each other – there should be

231

no medals, no awards, no commissions bestowed on a favoured few. Art must be free from government supervision or influence, free from intermediaries, like the academy, and free from privilege. We must entrust to artists alone the management of their interests. *Confier aux artistes seuls la gestion de leurs intérêts.*'

Well, I mean, I'm happy for the Communards but that's not po–

'Do you want to be managed by a gallery? By an institution? By a king?'

I didn't answer.

'Embarrassing.'

Gustave rummaged about in the glove compartment.

'Artists do not have to rely on the powerful for money *or* publicity.'

They definitely do.

'*C'est la honte!*'[41]

He flung a battered magazine at me.

'The committee published its own journal: *Officiel des arts*. It had essays on aesthetics and we invited all Communards to send in their opinions. We only asked that these submissions had the progress of art in mind.

41. It's embarrassing!

We also used the journal to publish the committee's accounts, minutes from meetings, budgets, receipts. We believed in full transparency.'

They entrusted artists, and only artists, with the management of their own interests . . .

'Your face! These ideas cannot be new to you? This happened in 1871.'

1871 . . . I felt sick. To know there was a time not so long ago when artists got what they wanted, I—

'La Commune did not last as long as we would have liked it to, but there were other reprises throughout history, before and after.'

I looked out of the car windows as Courbet failed to make the turn into Hyde Park and continued on past Lancaster Gate. He was stalling, and smoking, it was getting hard to see out of the windows.

'Take the Spanish Civil War, 1936 to 1939. Left-wing republicans fought right-wing nationalists – or fascists, depending on who you ask. The fascists had the army; the republicans had the unions. In 1930s Spain, those unions were led by anarchists. The CNT, Confederación Nacional del Trabajo, and the FAI, Federación Anarquista Ibérica. Anarcho syndicalists had spent the years leading up to the Civil War preparing for such an insurrection. Villagers had to pick up rifles and become soldiers, and people came from all over Europe to aid their fight against fascism in International Brigades, and I can see you zoning out . . .'

I'm not zoning out, I have somewhere to be.

'Not before you listen to me!'

I am not enjoying being attacked!

'Well, neither were the people of Barcelona, but they got on with it. A country may be in turmoil but life goes on as it always does. Most of Spain's economy was put under worker control. In Catalonia, the proletariat seized buildings, collectivized cafés, barbershops, hotels, restaurants, bootblack stands. Factories were run by the workers, and agrarian committees took over farming. In certain places, money was eliminated entirely. Decisions were made through councils of ordinary citizens. Of course, as art was an important part of everyday life, it was not exempt from collectivization. Theatres, cinemas, opera houses and cabaret were managed by the filmmakers and the dancers and the ushers, who were all members of the CNT. They constructed a cinema in a building that had once been a rotten bank. *They entrusted to artists alone the management of their interests. Say it with me now . . .*'

I could not imagine a world in which artists owned museums.

'And I am trying to show you that it is not difficult when revolutionaries have already achieved it!'

He was fully shouting at this point, but so was I.

'A life from each according to their ability, to each according to their need, as Karl Marx stated in 1875.'

But that's utopian! It isn't *real*!

'How would you know? Have you ever visited La place Vendôme?'

He was driving in a fast circle around the palace and he wouldn't let me go.

'There was once a statue of Napoleon atop a grand column in the 1st arrondissement – a column *he* erected to memorialize the 1805 Battle of Austerlitz, one of the many Napoleonic Wars. From up there, he looked down over the imperial dynasty he once conquered. Not only was it devoid of artistic value, but it was the egotistical portrait of a despotic ruler. People need to be emancipated, not ruled. The column did not belong in La Commune so we pulled Napoleon down.'

What do you mean, you pulled Napoleon down?

'Everyone likes to make such a fuss, as though change has to be complicated. *Ma chérie*, we got ropes, quarry workers, Communards, and we dragged the statue to his death. There was a mighty crash! Dust and smoke! It was violent and glorious, and I would do it again!'

People don't usually *brag* about being violent. You sound as bad as each other.

'Wha—'

Courbet pulled over on Bayswater Road, opened the car door, and the smoke clung to him as he stormed away. I had to chase him. I didn't want to be late.

'The *world* is violent! Constantly! Absolute monarchy is violent, money is violent, private property is violent, as are monuments that symbolize the state's love for violence. Any and all systems of power are based on brute force and violence. Look at this gentleman –' there was a man on the floor outside of Queensway tube station with a sign asking for money – 'Your precious government could organize the country so that nobody has to want for anything, but it chooses violence instead. How many die in police custody? How many sick people are left to rot? How many die trying to enter the country? You can't answer because it is easier for you to look away. But doing nothing is also violent. In fact, I would say it is worse, because it is a violence that believes itself to be innocent.'

He turned suddenly and I walked right into him. I didn't understand why he was upset. He said that the Commune's Federation of Artists was responsible for preserving monuments.

'Pieces of the statue were melted down to be made into coins for the new Republic. Destruction is not an end

236

point. The Russian revolutionary Comrade Mikhail Bakunin said as much when he declared that "the urge for destruction is also a creative urge". The Spanish revolutionary Comrade Buenaventura Durruti said, "we have no fear of ruins, we carry a new world, here in our hearts". The Spanish brigades could not fight the fascists from a moral high ground. Violence is an equal reaction to state-sanctioned violence! Sometimes what you *need* is an action that breaks the paralysis around the problem to prove change is not beyond our influence. Wasn't it Ursula K. Le Guin who once said: "We live in capitalism. Its power seems inescapable. So did the divine right of kings. Any human power can be resisted and changed by human beings. Resistance to change often begins in art."'

You weren't even alive at the same time.

'You do not know the divine right of ghosts! The problems you face are *not* fated. They are not an inexorable force and evil is not a biological law. Evil is made and the same evil can be destroyed. And violence –' he looked left and right to see if anybody was listening – 'can be a revolutionary action. Violence is a political tactic anarchists throughout history have used. The general strike, the boycott, protest, squatting, sabotage, arson, riot, assassination—'

I stepped back. Gustave, mate, I'm a fucking Muslim. I can't be casually chatting about terrorism on the street, or in the home, or anywhere.

'Don't be so childish. You think terrorism was invented in 2001? Throughout the nineteeth century, anarchists were a government's worst nightmare, and rightly so. If governments insist on installing themselves, maybe it is best if they live in fear of the people they claim to govern. Better than us living in fear of them, no? Violence in anarchism sometimes takes the name of *propagande par le fait*. Propaganda by the deed. Certainty makes it seem as if there's nothing we can do about our discontent. The anarchist does something that shocks people in order to catalyse revolution by shattering the illusion that this reality is fixed! In 1885, the *Chicago Tribune* wrote, *when a tramp asks you for bread, put arsenic on it and he will not trouble you anymore*. Lucy Parsons published a response in the same newspaper. It read: *Let every dirty, lousy tramp arm himself with a revolver or a knife, and lay in wait on the steps of the palaces of the rich and stab or shoot the owners as they come out. Let us kill them without mercy, and let it be a war of extermination.*'

I was speechless.

'No gods, no masters!'

No gods, no masters.

'The Art King is not any better than you or me. He is not worthy of more respect. He shouldn't decide the rules that you live by because there is nothing that qualifies him to rule over either of us, in the art world or out of it. He does not get to decide what is *certain*.'

I am not going to *kill* the Art King.

'I didn't tell you to.'

Gustave, I am not going to *kill* the Art King.

'That's up to you.'

The Art King

The gallery castle complex had archers along the battlements, and I waited in a long queue outside. The other guests were glamorous in the way that they looked, but also in the sense that they had their every need fulfilled. A man fanned a tarot deck in my face and I picked a card with a figure posing fancy and free on a cliff against a buttery yellow sky.

'The Fool! Delirious youth. You are walking out into the world to begin a new journey. Enjoy beginner's luck but be careful. If you continue unaware, you will topple straight off the edge of the world . . .'

I thought I knew what I was getting myself into, but when I got to the front of the queue, a man in a tunic shook his head and told me I was in the wrong line. He hurried me into a changing room where I found a rail of jester costumes. He said they were for the artists. A motley pattern in black and green to match the gallery's emblem, complete with matching curly toed slippers. The costume was itchy, and the bells on my toes were humiliating. I didn't want to leave the changing room, but the steward pushed me hard from behind and I tumbled like a doll into the court.

240

I looked up and saw only silver. The place was filled with silver people. They were *the super-rich*. Frosted white-blonde hair. There was a mist around them. I could literally smell it. Rich people smelt amazing. Or too amazing. They smelt excessive. The closer I got to the silver people, the more excessive I found them. I'd never seen anything like the rich, and in fact, I wanted to look at them more. I felt rewarded merely by looking. I hadn't felt anything in exhibitions for a long time, but I was feeling something now in the company of the Power 100.[42]

'I have to leave early tonight. I have a flight back to Oslo in the morning for the start of the hunting season.'

'Yes, but you sound acceptably Northern.'

'How can I be a fascist? I'm literally bisexual.'

'The recession is good for culture because it means the art schools will have to push their students into making commercially viable work again. They need to be teaching these artists to sell work for the art market, not market stalls.'

'Excuse me, excuse me. Can you stir the bubbles out of this champagne for me?'

---

42. Every year, the magazine *Art Review* publishes its ranking of the 100 most influential people in art. We have no idea why we haven't been on it yet. Having said that, we do not read *Art Review* to check. We also don't want to be on it.

'His new pieces are quite *blingy*. Street-influenced *Black* stuff.'

'She told me the gallery was closing in five minutes. I told her to bring me the manager.'

'Do they even *have* Waitrose outside of London?'

'I couldn't join the Ladies Who Lunch last week and I'm glad. The curator took them to galleries in *Shoreditch*. Can you *imagine*? So edgy.'

'The real issue preventing working-class youth from progressing in this day and age has nothing to do with money and everything to do with the fact they aren't taught Latin in school any more. They have no discipline.'

'If she doesn't have the money for the training required to become an opera singer, she should give up now.'

'Don't be silly, working-class people don't understand how to recycle.'

'I used to live in Brooklyn Heights in the 80s. It was very *Black*.'

'I didn't know about the *abuse*. I thought he was only harassing the interns.'

'She decides where we go on holiday. I decide when the war in Gaza ends.'

That's what I've been aiming for? Everything sounded pre-written. They were villains, they were racist, they hated the masses; and they thought they were in charge of our fate. The jester costume was making me sweat buckets, so I went to the back of the court to lean on a wall. I thought I was going to faint.

'The trick is to wear a T-shirt underneath. Trust me, I've been coming long enough. I'm practically *clinging* on.'

There was another jester on the wall. Old, tall, visibly drunk.

'What are you doing back here? You're a shiny, young thing. You should be up front with the rest of them . . .'

She gestured across the square where a bunch of artists were doing cartwheels in front of the empty red throne where the King was due to arrive at some point during the night.

'First time?'

I nodded.

'Then I shall be your guide. Tonight is a fundraiser for the gallery, but it is so much more than that. You enter the court through whatever means or magic you happen upon, and once you're in, you have to behave like a good courtier. Be correct in your decorum. Attend to power. Juggle! Cartwheel! Dance for your dinner! It sounds ridiculous, but art has always been so tied up in its own formality. The nobility says *come in, come in*. Because, think about it, you can't have someone outside the court saying the King's a wanker. You have to bring him inside and get him to say it to the King's face. Then it's *allowed* to be funny.'

She wasn't laughing.

'At least we get to call ourselves artists.'

She clinked our glasses together and I downed my drink. The jester had her arm around me, consoling a younger version of herself, like a drunk auntie at a wedding or a funeral.

'You do realize we're pawns. We're being moved around the board for *their* benefit. Work sells, work gets flipped. Artists have to watch it happen, and the house always wins.'

My eyes were still adjusting to the silver light glinting off everything. Who *were* these people?

'They're the funding class. Art has always been at the mercy of the aristocracy, and this lot were born into it. They are invited to court because the gallery needs money to stay in business. What the gala is doing tonight is networking through them, pursuing donors. These people run foundations, or they have extensive social circles they can draw on. A lot of them work in PR. There's a big overlap there. Putting people together like this is their social and professional role – or not professional. It's a professionalism that belongs in the same category as a gentleman's hand-shake. This is an event on the social calendar where they can exercise their social influence and they come in droves because this is what they were hothoused to do. It might look like they're having fun, but it's basically a Bacardi advert – stage-managed. They're actually on the clock.'

I *hated* them. I hated the court. I hated how much I had wanted to come inside the gates. I moved on to my third drink.

'Yeah, but the food is actually hot. That's how you know they've got good catering. I do love an event. I love the spectacle of something like this.'

I didn't know how she could love anything about this.

'It's not important that we like the people here; it's important that they like us. Their politics are not going to be our politics. Their ethics are not going to be our ethics. Although, there are artists I know who are fascinated by these characters and will talk to them just for the experience.'

I don't want to go anywhere near them. I don't appreciate the opportunity to be in the room while they get to be obnoxious.

'Me neither. I'm good back here. I don't want to get stuck in their orbit.'

But you still came?

'My agent ordered me to. At least it's not a *private dinner*. Whose dinner isn't private? She told me to be seen and not heard.'

Why aren't you allowed to speak?

'There are a lot of collectors here, and I get myself in trouble. A collector once told me which work he owned, and I said, *oh, that was the only one left after all the good ones had gone*. I used to ask collectors how much they'd spend on my works without showing them a price list, and the answer could be anywhere from five to fifty thousand.'

I was not used to hearing those numbers.

'Collectors aren't bankrupting themselves for their unbelievable passion for the arts – fifty grand for these people is like fifty quid to us. They can afford it in the same way we can afford a new jumper.'

I actually couldn't process this information – and then Princess Eugenie walked past.

'She's a director at Hauser & Wirth, you know.'

Of course she is. I wanted to obliterate everything. I wanted to go back to a time when art was the by-product of human culture and not an opportunistic industry built around something that used to be sincere. If I lived in a cave and finger-painted the outlines of animals to track the lunar cycle, I think I would be a lot happier.

'This is what it does to you. We get into art thinking it is going to be such a fulfilling life, but art is all closed doors.'

Caves don't have doors.

'Caves don't have doors!'

We got more drinks.

'You don't want to know what's going on *behind* gallery doors. Arms-dealing industrialists, Big Pharma, money laundering, enclosure of the commons, *old money*, which is a polite way of saying slave-trade profiteering. The gallery is corrupt! But the heartbreak is our own fault. We assume art is a moral act, even if that isn't fair. Artists aren't priests, and curators aren't bishops, and galleries were never meant to showcase morality. They are businesses, not temples. This gallery probably believes tonight's gala is an adjunct to what they do but actually it is the heart of who they are.'

This really was the end, wasn't it? Gustave was right. Mo was too. Valentine. Daisy. Sangita. Amelia on Jupiter. I didn't want this money from these people.

'That one's a collector.'

A small woman went past.

'I've spoken to her before. It was horrible. There was something so needy and dejected about her. She was like a gloomy weather front coming your way, like, ah fuck. You know when you're talking to someone and you realize, *you're not in a good way, are you*? There's something awry within you. Maybe she liked art once upon a time but her grasp of art has become so completely abstracted since she placed herself so high up on the food chain. The King is a collector, of course. Last week, he was passing through one of his museums during install, and he asked a technician why the colour of the white paint that had just been put on the walls was darker than the white paint on the opposite wall. The technician had to explain that it was because the paint was *wet.*'

She stamped her foot and the bells on her slippers jangled.

'Collectors aren't a homogeneous bunch by any measure. They can go from very naive to hard-noses who know more about art than a lot of curators; and I've met small-timers in other cities who are even *nice.* They simply want to invest in their local scene because they know they are one of the few people who can do so. In London, it's mostly people who care about art only so long as it is useful to their social standing, and that woman who passed us earlier – I know for a fact she has a flat in Helsinki dedicated to her glass collection. I went there once, and it has museum-quality cabinets and the pieces are lit perfectly.'

I probably wouldn't be so sad if I had enough money to buy a flat in Helsinki to display my glass collection.

'One of the worst things the rich have done is make us believe that aesthetics belong to them. Part of that belief relies on the conflation of aesthetics as being intrinsically linked with money and power, giving it an

248

ethical slant. You must know that feeling – *I can't have that because it's nice, and I'm an ethical person so nice things are not for me.* But you're allowed to have nice things without compromising your values. Everybody deserves beauty in their lives. The worst collectors are the ones that buy up all the beautiful artworks and keep their collections to themselves. Or no –' she pointed back at the small woman – 'the worst collectors want to own a little bit of the artist's soul; because owning *you* means getting close to your *mystique*.'

That creeped me out.

'I used to see it when I was a younger artist, how collectors would present their charm to me, as if they needed *me* to acknowledge *them*. They needed me to like them back. It was a bit like a mating ritual. I had to manipulate the outcome of the interaction to make the collector, or the curator, think it was their idea to include my art in their plans. Everyone involved in art is seeking affirmation, whether it's a *wow, that painting truly resonates with me*, or a *you've got really good taste*, or a *well done, you, for buying something, oh, you're a good little collector, aren't you?* The collector, in particular, wants the approval of the artist because they're going to be living with the work, and they're building a mythic idea of who you are.'

I didn't want to cultivate mystique any more. If anything, I wanted to cultivate irrelevance.

'Cheers to that.'

249

The jester asked if I had collectors. I told her most of my sales had actually happened through Instagram – and I cringed as I said it, and in doing so, I felt how much I had internalized this *proper way of doing things.* I was acting like that tutor who had judged me in university for selling any work at all.

'You are a novelty to the court. It doesn't even matter what you're making as long as it's coming to them in a way they haven't seen before. Social media isn't new but they are sheltered. There's a novelty for them in engaging with any tribe outside their own. That's partly why they have an interest in art, because they believe it is a way they can expand their experience. If being educated is akin to being rich, and if knowing about the world makes you look clever, you can see why they would want to get up close and personal to someone *authentic.* It makes them look well travelled. Never mind that knowledge is created everywhere by everyone; these people collect art for the same reason they develop and gentrify areas full of immigrant-run businesses – they want the restaurants to stay, but they don't want the Black and brown people to carry on living there. It's white expansion. It's extractive. Collectors want a sip of that bohemian glamour. They want to be part of a groovy, creative scene. It's a positive discrimination initiative. *People like you* make *their* dreams come true.'

That made me self-conscious in the precise way I never wanted to feel.

'It doesn't matter if, say, a white collector says he *really* connects with a brown woman's self-portrait. These people are so self-enamoured that everything connects back to them. They're looking for self-reflection in art. It's this very narcissistic desire to accumulate, and that accumulation increases their wealth, not just financial, but the wealth of who they are. That is the economy of the relationship between collector and artist. Listen, it's nice to earn a living but it's almost like you end up making work *for* this horrible person who you'd never want to break bread with. Artworks are trophies to these people, like the mounted head of a stag. It's very *royal*. It's very Great Gatsby or – what's that film? *Human Centipede.*'

I didn't think I had a choice in how this all played out, because I was born to be an artist and that innate desire made me beg for the right to be myself. I wanted to be an artist more than anything, but I was wrong for thinking that. I didn't want to be an artist. I wanted to make art. I thought the only way I could make art was if I did it full-time, and even if that is true, I didn't want to carry on down this route if it led to the court. It was time to leave.

I wasn't about to go near the silver people, so I inched my way around the walls. I didn't make it very far before slipping on something and face-planting the grass. The jester caught up with me. The grass below was darker than grass should be.

'It's the heads.'

I hadn't noticed from the outside but the archers weren't alone on the battlements. There were spikes, and skewered on to them, bloody heads. It was too dark to make out their faces, but I felt my body clench. The waitstaff, as beautiful as the patrons and probably models and actors themselves, were busy mopping fresh blood as it rained around the edges of the party.

'They're the critics.'

I couldn't look at them.

'You know how it is. The industry repels and—'

Compels us all.

'There's a tension there; a dialectic that is harnessed by creative practitioners as a means of production. It's very difficult to be an artist, and it can be quite profitable to make art about the uphill climb. The institution likes to think it's in on the joke. But art is pretty amenable to having the piss taken out of it, because art wants us to challenge its own status quo. Some artists spend their careers screaming at Mummy and Daddy: *You don't understand me! Oh, and by the way, can you lend me a tenner? I need to buy cigs.* We like to believe we are rebellious, when in fact we're a bunch of middle-class professionals, and we're much more orthodox than we would like to admit. It's like Nam June Paik said, *An artist should always bite the hand that feeds it – but not too hard!*'

I knew what she was describing because I had made QT the perfect courtier.

'But the heads up there bit the whole hand off.'

The jester took a napkin and began dabbing the blood off me. I wanted it to be fake. I wanted it to be wet paint.

'Or they tried to.'

A group of knights marched past. There were quite a few sirs and dames in attendance; artists who had received their royal honours, where the sword had bounced over their head instead of cutting straight through it.

'It's reassuringly bohemian to be a *bit* badly behaved but there comes a point when the court won't take it any more. The court wants our respect. It wants us to go through it. If you go *around*, it's the *wrong* thing to do. You *can* be outrageous, but you can't be plain rude. You can't do anything that seriously embarrasses these people because their reputation is everything to them. So, once a year, the executioner rounds up the thinkers who pose a real threat to the imperial art system. Anybody who gets close to neutralizing the value systems that mean people can hold power over each other.'

But how would they even achieve that?

'As we've spoken about tonight, these tyrants have an insatiable appetite to constantly be accumulating. What if that appetite was itself a weakness?'

What are you saying?

'What if you were to take that moment of accumulation and you could insert something into the non-perceptive mechanisms of the art elite – into the very *way* that they are . . .'

I don't get what you're saying.

'I'm saying that there's no way you could stand up to these people and their entrenched, archaic systems and expect to win in a toe-to-toe fight. Not you on your own. But you could create something. Something that is dangerous and poisonous and clever, and you could insert it into their system like a virus. It could kill them from the inside. They wouldn't expect it. Some germ that spreads from collector to curator to gallery to museum, some proxy thing that mutates wildly and infects them, something they appropriate into them-selves, and which totally knocks their oppressive behaviours right out.'

You need to tell me what that thing could be.

'Well, the critics know an exhibition review isn't going to do it. These museums, this castle, the King, your compulsion to make art, even the very fact we are alive and having this conversation, and in these costumes no less – it's all nonsense, and there's no sensible way of *writing* about anything non-sensible without it becoming sensible again – because you have to use sense to communicate it, and then the whole critique falls apart,

254

because what you're talking about is an experience that is not containable within rationality. I think it would have to be an artwork. But I can't tell you what that is and neither can they.'

She looked up again.

'The sad thing is, a lot of these people can't bear to live in a world as far gone as this one, and when the executioner comes round, he finds they've already done his job for him.'

She spat on the floor.

'And the court puts them on display.'

My stomach was in knots.

'What tarot card did you pull, by the way?'

The Fool, I think?

'Do you know much about Shakespeare? He loved his fools. They were tricksters who would outwit the higher-ups, but they were functional too, setting the pace and moving the story along. The fools were the only ones who could see what was really going on.'

At that moment, floodlights and horns roused the courtyard.

'He's here.'

The silver crowd split in two, a red carpet rolled out, and a generic-looking white man with massive bags under his eyes made his way through the court. I watched him shaking hands and forcing smiles when the jesters showed him their party tricks. I watched everyone trying their best to win this man's approval and felt only second-hand embarrassment for still being amongst them. Before I left, I let myself take the whole scene in so that I was sure I would never forget just how bad this moment felt. I could see every detail under the light: the bloody floor under high heels, tired staff under chess-piece topiary, the castle walls under critics' heads and – one of the heads, his hair was long now, and he was a writer, and I thought we were going to collaborate one day, because I thought he knew the way out.

Mo.

'Poor artist.'

I think I was screaming, and then there was this man standing too close to me, far too fucking close, the way men always do. The King's eyes were black and I could smell his rancid breath. I thought he must be rotten inside, but I felt rotten too. I stuck two fingers down my throat and vomited into his gaping mouth. The deed was done and I still felt bad. I thought about how Mo was always good.

Afterlife

During the 1880s, Arnold Böcklin created five versions of the same painting, *The Isle of the Dead*. In the image, rocks enclose a dark grove of cypress trees on an island far across the sea. The water and the trees are totally still as a small rowing boat arrives on the shores. The scene is based on the English Cemetery in Florence, which was close to Böcklin's studio at the time, and where Böcklin's baby girl was buried at just seven months old.

In 1991, Félix González-Torres created a portrait of his partner, Ross Laycock, the same year Ross died from complications due to AIDS. The portrait took the form of seventy-nine kilograms of sweets in colourful wrappers in a heap in the corner of a room; the weight implied a body, implied Ross. Whenever the work is restaged, audiences are invited to take sweets directly from the installation. The artwork would gradually disappear over the course of an exhibition except the artist stipulated curators could replenish the pile continuously, and so they do.

Chris Ofili's huge painting *No Woman, No Cry* from 1998 depicts Doreen Lawrence in profile. She is drawn between a lattice of patterns that resemble a chain-link fence. She is crying. Her son Stephen was murdered in a racist attack in London five years before the work was made, and in each of Doreen's tears is a small photograph of him. The tears curl right off her face, down the curve of her neck and around her shoulder. He clings to her.

After the 2011 Norway attacks in which seventy-seven people were killed, Jonas Dahlberg's proposal for a memorial was selected from an international open call. Dahlberg suggested making a physical cut through the peninsula facing the island of Utøya where the massacre took place. Water would flow through the open wound, and the land would always gape. It was too acute a symbol for some residents – a memorial that would recall the memory too strongly – and in the end, the proposal never went ahead.

In 2022, the artist Lizzy Rose died from the impact of severe Crohn's disease. The next year, her friends organized a retrospective of her work that stretched across galleries in Margate. There were prints of stranded whales – creatures who produce the floating gold of ambergris in their bowels; there was a self-portrait taken in the bath alongside a caption about Rose's constant thirst; and an exhibition of living moss that was art's job to keep alive.

Mum

Mo was gone. I needed to move on.

'What does moving on look like?'

Being reborn in a different body with someone else's straightforward dream, applying for a job, getting the job, and never setting foot in a gallery again.

'I thought this was about Mohammed?'

It had been six months since I'd moved back home. Mum was over what she was calling my *performance*.

'If it's not about Mohammed, what is it?'

Mum came with me to the funeral. I thought I'd done all my crying, but then I went to the Janazah and saw Mrs Kelly. It *was* about Mo, of course it was, but it was also about what he taught me. Art was a cult of personality where everyone auditioned to be the next unique individual. I auditioned with them, imbuing objects with my conceptual labour and hoping for the best. But I shouldn't have been thinking of myself. There was something deeply humiliating about committing to an ideology that could fix the world while I was very much stuck on the couch. It didn't matter that most artists earnt fuck all, even the *good* ones. It didn't matter that art wasn't necessary to the functioning wheels of society. I didn't want a wage or a society, and art was still necessary to me. I just wanted a world that would have kept Mo alive. Without him, I'd rather die.

'First off, if you die, I'll kill you. Second, Quest, be serious.'

This *is* serious. Being an artist is about a serious commitment to a creative practice and I've got nothing to show for myself. I'm going to have to retrain, do something useful. This world isn't safe for real artists.

'What are you going to do, then?'

I'm going to become a dental hygienist! Because none of this is real. None of it matters. This is stuff someone else gave mattering to. Art, money, power; who gets to have a career, who doesn't. We just created meaning around these things, which *means* we can also destroy it.

'What's wrong with you?'

You raised me.

'You should have gone to drama school, not art school.'

We were glaring at each other. I was being awful.

'Let me get this right. You're saying that because you don't have a career, you are going to stop making art altogether and whiten people's teeth?'

I had painted myself into a corner and that corner was Henry Fuseli's *The Nightmare*.

'Do you really think that because no one ever overheard me singing in a pub and signed me, I should have quit singing?'

Nani taught Mum folk songs when she was younger. She has a really beautiful voice. She sings on the way to work, when she's cooking, and when she's serving lunch to the kids. They sing along in broken Bengali even though they haven't got a clue what she's saying. They're so charmed, meaning is beside the point.

'Are you waiting for me to say, Quest, your art is so important! You can't quit! The world would be worse off without it!'

This woman was supposed to be my mother.

'I don't get it. I thought you knew what you were getting yourself into. The world doesn't owe you anything because you want to be an artist. It owes you plenty as a *citizen*. But as an artist? You're acting like you have been hard done by but you chose this, and you have to take responsibility. What did you think was going to happen?'

I felt winded.

'No, really, what did you think was going to happen?'

If I put in enough time and effort, one day I would be able to support myself.

'But you didn't always think that. You never attached a grand narrative to art, not at first anyway. You just *made* it.'

Yeah?

'You are allowed to just *make* things, you know. I won't tell.'

I could imagine Mo agreeing. I could imagine Mo telling me that a creative practice and a career were two very different things.

'Before you left home, you had a sketchbook in your hand at all times. There were always scribbles on the couch because you'd keep pencils in your back pockets. The lamp was always on in your room, and not because you needed light to sleep, but because you would fall asleep drawing. Now, you only ever have your phone in your hand.'

I closed my eyes and sighed.

'Like, that, right there. How much energy are you wasting moping around? Take that energy back. Use it to actually *make* something if you love art as much as you say you do. It's what Mo would have wanted.'

That hurt.

'I just think you need to find the bit of yourself that you started with, back before this careerism shite got to your head. What would thirteen-year-old Quest say if she could see you now? Or no, what would *you* say to *her*?'

I wasn't interested in myself any more. I was sick of myself.

'OK, well, imagine this. In two years' time, you're sitting on a bench and – tell me the name of an important art person.'

Mrs Kelly.

'Not what I was expecting, but OK. *Two* years have passed. You're sitting on a bench in Princes Park and Mrs Kelly is walking her Lhasa Apso. She sits down and says, *How's it going? I heard you moved back home. Are you still making art?'*

I would tell her—

'No, speak as though you're on the bench right now. You're not in the living room. I'm not here. *Go.'*

I am . . . still making art. It's the thing I care most about. For a minute, things were tenuous. I was a worker who performed the role of artist and I became alienated from the very thing I enjoyed. It almost completely gouged me. But my body made the decision a long time ago that art is how I will live. I allowed myself to take a break, which is fine because an art practice is an entire life. I needed to remind myself of that. I needed to make an effort to recognize that thing in me that is picked up and connected across the years and the places and the people that I am.

'And who are you now?'

Someone who makes art. Someone who doesn't care about being known as an artist, or being *known* at all. No artist is made *real* by commercial or institutional success, but only by this need inside of us to create. I had entered university thinking it was going to be one long art lesson, until I heard a gun on the starting line and felt the surge of everybody running forward. I went along with them. I had this idea that if I stopped running, I'd fail. I needed to slow down to figure out why we were all running in the first place. When I gave myself a fallow year, it was because I needed to figure out what I actually wanted to say with my art, if anything. It was a return to childhood. I drew sunsets and trees and old tins of soup that had been in Nani's cupboards since before I was born. I didn't show anyone what I'd made and I looked on that as a halcyon period.

'And did you . . . work during this time?'

Yes, but I didn't care about how I made something as trivial as money. The job itself didn't matter because the art mattered so much more. I wouldn't even know what to do with too much money. I wouldn't go on holiday. I wouldn't buy a new outfit. I'd be on that holiday, in that new outfit, uneasy because I don't really care about those things. They aren't going to give me anything. Art is the only thing that can offer me something, because that's where the beauty and the optimism comes in, and the *clarity*, and the way out of all this heavy certainty. I went to exhibitions and I felt myself come back into my body.

'Oh, that's brilliant, Quest. But you said that you didn't show anybody what you were making – is that still the case?'

I think it is sad that art only assumes value when it is tied to display. It's like everyone needs to be doing art in view of the public, and the online public, for it to count. I watched other people exhibiting constantly and it didn't seem to add much depth to an artist's practice, only their wallet. That's sad too. Artists are such a productive force. There's this feeling that in making art, you're somehow changing the world materially. The same can't be said for galleries. Galleries have an administrative role, and that's all. Artists produce talent and galleries absorb that force, so it's a wonder galleries treat artists so badly. They *need* us. I didn't want to let anybody treat me badly, and Mo showed me I don't need permission to do things. I can just do them. So I've let go of other people's ideas of how I should live my life, and I've been making art for myself.

'End scene.'

Mum was smiling. I wasn't going to pay her mortgage off because of this decision.

'That would be nice but I've known you your whole life so I've never expected that to happen.'

You should have had another kid, a really sensible one.

'I like the one I've got, thank you very much.'

I felt my voice lifting.

'So, what is going to happen now?'

I want to be in community with other people who feel this way.

'How might you break that down into smaller goals so you can build a structure you can definitely work towards?'

I can start by putting myself on a waiting list for a studio space. They're cheaper up here.

'Do you want me to see if there's any work going in school?'

Yes, please. As long as you're OK with me living here for a bit, or a while.

'If that's what it takes for you to survive.'

That night, I emailed a studio group. The very next day, they replied telling me they had been trying to get in touch for months; a studio member had named me as his replacement, and I must know him, his name was Mohammed, and they were very sorry to hear that he had died.

Sheila

A twenty-minute walk from the city centre, past car dealerships, tyre piles and empty lots, there was a 90s office building under the property guardianship of artists. Licensed on a monthly rolling contract, the rough blue office carpet could have been pulled out from under them at any moment for redevelopment. But the walk was too long, and the crime rate was high, and the heating didn't work in the building anyway, so it remained the cherished, wretched home of a studio group.

Sheila must have been in her sixties. She was wearing a denim apron and there was a bright orange stick of Blackpool rock in one pocket. She took me on a tour through the warren, where each studio was a chipboard hutch under a suspended ceiling of missing tiles. There was a skip by the entrance full of scrap wood, most of the toilets were out of order and the kitchen was nuclear – but she was happy.

'Here we are.'

We had arrived at Mo's studio – my studio – but I was too nervous to go inside.

'You have the key now. You can come back when you're ready.'

I nodded without saying anything.

'Do you want to come and see mine so you can get an idea of the size? I say that but I knocked the wall down so I could share it with my partner, John. He's an artist too. A piss artist.'

She laughed. Their studio was an organized mess of wires, yarn, clay and musical instruments. There was a desktop computer, a drafting desk, bookshelves, and a loom that divided the room in two opposite a large mirror.

'You weave from behind so I need to know what it's looking like on the front.'

Sheila sat me on a couch that folded out into a futon and turned Radio City on. She said the studios were a home away from home when there was something going on in a studio member's life. On the tour, she told me not everyone here was an artist. There was also a seamstress, a dancer, a beekeeper, a poet and a bunch of graphic designers.

'Come to the next reading group if you want? You can meet them there.'

I had seen it advertised on the noticeboard in the corridor next to posters about a fundraiser, a Christmas market, crits, a member's exhibition and a donation request for a food bank.

'The reading group is the first Wednesday of the month, and we're halfway through something called *The*

268

Hologram. Have you read it? It was written by the artist Cassie Thornton. Mo actually requested it but we didn't get round to it before . . .'

I hadn't heard of it.

'The premise is basically: what if people organized themselves into groups of four, and they met regularly, and three of them focused their attention on the fourth, and they considered the fourth person's mental, physical and social health. Are they doing OK? Are there any thorns they need pulling out? How might they go about yanking those thorns? The team of three aren't trained as doctors or therapists or anything, they learn on the job based on the needs of the fourth person, who gets called the hologram, and who teaches the three how to care for them, while also learning how they need to be cared for. Everyone is the hologram for another group of three, and that way, we create a network in which we are all held.'

QT would never have happened if I'd been a hologram.

'Mo requested it because he thought it would be a good reminder that we can organize ourselves in any shape we want to. God, he loved it here.'

She rummaged on the shelf, and I tried not to cry.

'I'll lend you John's copy, and he can have mine. This world isn't very good at enabling care. It's *great* at enabling violence. But art might be where we learn how to look after the rest of the world. It's nice to have a group where we can do that imagining together. But if you don't fancy reading something, there's a crit on Thursday if you're up for it?'

I wanted to be making art and communicating around it, but I hadn't even got around to the first part yet.

'Oh, come anyway. People get excited when there's someone new because it means fresh eyes on the work – and when you have that genuine peer-review, or even better, a longevity in your relationship with other creatives who can think through the work as it changes over the years, it can make you believe you're making art that *means* something in the world, because at least one other person is working to understand that meaning.'

Yeah, when it's not just a conversation but being *in conversation*, and you can feel your ideas moving forward.

'You're pulling in their references and perspectives, and together, you're giving the work a dressing-down so that you can see what it is and what it's doing.'

She chewed on her rock.

'I really don't mean to ambush you or your schedule but the Christmas market is also happening soon.'

I must have made a face.

'Now, now. I know there are people who think art can only be good if it is *fine art* and it is about *a relationship with the canon*, not *Christmas*. But you should make something. The lads in the garage down the road always come to get stuff for their wives. People love the market. *I* love the market. Art should be a normal, affordable thing. I like selling normal work to normal people at reasonable prices – people who are going to put it up in their house and actually *look at it.*'

I thought she was asking me to make Christmas cards, but she showed me pictures from last year's market and most of the items on sale were just art.

'The home is such an undervalued space for building a relationship with an artwork. Liverpool has so many galleries, and that's great, because it gives us the privilege of building relationships with artworks in the permanent collections that last our entire lives. We continue to change, and the artwork stays the same, but maybe it gives us something different every time. Great! But there are images that mean even more to me than the ones in museums. For instance, I used to stay at my friend's grandparents' house all summer over in Blackpool. They'd put me in a tiny bedroom in the attic where the only decor was this one painting on the wall in a cheap frame.'

She went back to the shelves.

'I found out later it was a print of *Holy Mountain, I* by Horace Pippin. He was an American artist born in 1888.'

She opened the book on to a page with a painting of a forest. In the foreground, there was a shepherd surrounded by lounging animals. A lion, a goat, a wolf, a jaguar. One or two of the animals had been pulled straight from the artist's imagination, and all of them seemed totally at peace. The dark grass was thick and mottled with bright daisies.

'They must have put it up because it was a sleepy scene with animals, so it was good for a kid's bedroom. But Horace Pippin taught himself how to paint after he got shot in the shoulder during the First World War. I didn't know that when I was ten. All I knew was what the image told me. I didn't have a phone or a tablet, *Holy Mountain, I* is what I would look at, and if you look closely, you'll see the tiny soldiers with guns running through the trees in the background, which used to scare the living daylights out of me in that attic.'

She leant over my shoulder.

'I've probably spent longer looking at that painting, and longer thinking about it, than I have all the masterpieces in all the museums in the world. The fantasy surrounding the shepherd while the soldiers charge. The artist's ability to create fantasy around them while, still, the soldiers charge. This man had PTSD from the war. A gunshot wound left his right arm disabled. The US only abolished slavery in 1865, about twenty years before he was born. It's no wonder there was violence in the background. The painting might be unreal but it's certainly honest. It had a massive influence on my work –' her tapestry was decorated with the same flowers – 'and so I have a lot of appreciation for whoever decided to buy it from a carbootie.[43] If you think about it, I might never have seen it otherwise, because it's not in our museums.'

She was right about the Christmas market. I was still deconditioning.

'And at the risk of sounding like a nutter, there's a performative aspect to all forms of art. There's the performance of the artist who makes the piece. Think of all the energy Horace Pippin charged that painting with, and then imagine me, fifty-odd years ago, standing in the place where the artist once stood during the original performance. The energy can come back out. The artwork creates a direct line back to the artist. It creates an exchange between the audience and the maker. That's how art connects us to each other. I don't hold back any work in the hopes a collector's going to be knocking round these parts. I want to sell my work at the Christmas market because it means becoming closer to my own people.'

I told her I'd make something. I didn't know what, but I was done making art in the hope of influencing people. I wanted to relate to them instead, and I didn't know how much I should sell it for.

'You could do the man-hours thing?'

43. Scouse for car boot sale.

Sheila picked up a new bobbin to weave the next part of the tapestry in a different colour.

'How much is an hour of your time worth and how many did it take? I could tell you one of my pieces is priced at sixty quid an hour, and that would be acceptable as a highly skilled tradesperson, but it might not be acceptable in the context of the postcode. A degree might add to your worth? I don't know. I never did one. My vases are downstairs in the kiln, and I learnt the basics in evening classes a long time ago. I was on the dole and students paid 45p per pound of finished work. It was back when people could smoke inside. We'd put on these quick exhibitions and at the end of the night, my pots would be full of cigarettes.'

I would have fumed.

'It's not going to hurt them. They're pots. They've been through the *fire*! Other artists price things by adding up the cost of materials so they're not out of pocket. I sometimes make work out of rubbish, though. I go to second-hand shops and collect shells off the beach in New Brighton. I can't walk past a demolished house without having a rummage.'

Her studio was full of these trinkets. She seemed to do a bit of everything.

'Materials don't come into the equation when I'm deciding on prices, because I think no matter what it's made of, somebody confronted with a piece of art consciously or unconsciously responds to the human achievement in effort. Not that I make work to sell it. This is just to give you some ideas.'

I asked her to remind me when the crit was, and the Christmas market. I'd got into the habit of keeping a pocket-sized notepad on me at all times because I didn't feel *good* when I went on my phone.

'Get a phone box!'

She pointed across the room at a box nailed next to the light switch.

'When I arrive, I put my phone in there and I don't take it out until I leave. You have to make the studio a product-ive thinking space, not just a *doing* space; and you wouldn't expect an athlete to start running without stretching first. One sec, this is a heddle. If I pull it –' a section of vertical warp stretched towards us – 'it lets me get the bobbin through a bit faster.'

I wanted her to teach me everything she knew.

'It's all about owning your own process and deciding what structure you want in your day. Whether you want to go it alone, or keep the door open for a gab.'

When Sheila had shown me around, she'd pointed out the do-not-disturb signs that could be hooked on to door handles.

'In my other job, I work as a lab technician, and there are days when I won't utter a single word until I come home for dinner. So, when it comes to my time in the studio, I want there to be a social element. John's the complete opposite. He's worked in a pub ever since we met, which means his face-to-face time is at a premium. He doesn't want to bring people into the studio because that's the one thing that he's got that's just for him. We avoid coming in at the same time, but that's easy enough. John is one of those people who gets totally absorbed in a project for six months and then reads books for the rest of the year, and then he'll go on tour with a band, and – he gets self-conscious about that sometimes.'

About what?

'Doing a mix of things. Not being that visible around the studios. But no one is waiting here to punish him. He gets in such a huff, and I say, *John, it might take someone thirty years to make a drawing but they're an artist as much as the person who makes thirty drawings in a day.* That usually shuts him up. I hate this assumption that everything you do should feed into a single rolling ball of momentum, when the good thing about art is there are no rules. He sometimes says to me he wants to set himself studio days. Why would you give yourself a regime? Let yourself live. There are enough expectations of us in life. We're supposed to study hard, work even harder, have a family, get rich—'

Do you two have any kids?

'Neither of us ever wanted them, we weren't interested in compromising on our time – we couldn't. We've taken thirty years learning how to get into each other's heads on a personal level, the way any couple might, but we've also spent that time getting closer to the creative side of the other person, and it's a side that is much more vulnerable in my experience. We both love art more than anything else, even each other, and we didn't want to take on a responsibility that would get in the way, if we could help it.'

She stopped weaving.

'I want to be able to put my phone in that box and not have to worry that someone is relying on me. Within the belief system of our relationship, committing ourselves to our practices is what we need to do to be happy alone *and* together. If I wasn't with another artist, the person would get sad about me not prioritiz-ing them. But I don't think I could, or that I should have to. I'm so glad we found each other. That sounds quite harsh, doesn't it?'

I thought it sounded romantic.

'Even though I might not be able to predict what he's going to make next, we're always in agreement about what he *should* make. We get to have these really valuable conversations about what we're each working on, and sometimes he becomes a surrogate or a test space when I need help solving problems, and I get to do the same for him. Art drives me crazy sometimes. It

277

would be so much worse if a non-art partner had no idea why I'd gone mad for a week. It'd feel like they weren't seeing a fundamental part of me.'

Sheila retrieved a bobbin and started shuffling it back and forth through the warp, keeping one eye on the mirror and the other on her handiwork. I was thinking of the young relationship I'd had with Mo, and the one we could have had here in the studios; I was thinking about the young relationship I'd had with art, and how there was still time to make things right between us.

'It's not quite looking right.'

It looked great.

'You have this idea of how you hope a piece will come out, and that concept is always a golden, fuzzy, abstract, perfect vision *because* it doesn't exist yet so it *can* be perfect. Then there's that terrible journey from the initial idea to the outcome. All downhill. You end up with something that's nowhere near the lovely golden thing you dreamt of, and you have to deal with that tragedy. But it's always nice hearing from people who can't ever know what you were aiming for, and I don't *really* care because I enjoy it too much. Did you know decorative tapestries predate painting on canvas? Linen weaves were found in pharaoh's tombs, but we had to wait until the fourteenth century for canvas. Yeah, I love weaving. It feels like a core human experience to create something like this. The people of old must have been so satisfied. When I come to the studio, I feel like an ancient woman who has woken up and set herself the goal of tilling a field, and she's achieved it! And thus she sleeps the especially refreshing and comfortable sleep of someone who's done what she set out to do.'

She got up and started going through her records.

'There's a gospel song . . . here it is, by Pastor T. L. Barrett and the Youth for Christ Choir called "Like a Ship . . . (Without a Sail)". The choir sings "we did our work today" and they repeat it for the full four minutes.'

She set it playing.

'That line used to make me weep. Back before I had a studio, when I was working full-time in the lab – when I didn't get to do the work I wanted to do – I could feel this enormous, anxious pressure building up that took the form of all the art I hadn't made. Because I was still having the ideas, but that part of me was generating and percolating and doing its thing behind my eyeballs while I was existing in various places between work and the train and the kitchen. That pressure became the motivating force. I could feel the avalanche of material waiting to be let loose and I knew it was going to be a great release . . .'

Did it work?

'Did what work?'

Did you feel a release?

'I think that song will always make me cry, but yes, it worked. I reduced my hours and started renting this place, which felt very formal after years of breaking into spaces – but that's a story for another time.'

She winked.

'All I ever wanted was a daily practice. I come here after work so that I can have that daily *commune*. Even if I'm knackered, I want to commune with the material. That's the bit I consider to be the art, never mind the object that gets created. No, it is the practical fact that I am allowed to do art. The communing is the art, and the rest is bullshit.'

That's all any of us want.

'I feel like a teenager when I'm here. A studio is close in spirit to a teenager's bedroom because it's where someone gets to be obsessed with whatever they want, and no one bats an eye because a teenager's role is to have obsessions. I hyperfixate to the point I forget about everything else to a dangerous level. *I don't need dinner, I don't need a wee.* That's an issue because ceramics, for example, is all about waiting around but I'll want that clay ready *now*! I always have lots of projects on the go so I have a way of getting that energy out of me, like a negative charge shooting to earth in a big mad flash of lightning.'

The record ended.

'Come with me.'

We passed Mo's studio and I squeezed the key in my pocket. Sheila was taking me to the kiln so I could see what she was planning on putting in the members' exhibition. She told me to lower my expectations, she'd had some disasters in the past, but she was giddy as she said it.

'I use organic processes and the materials fight back. Colour is the bane of my existence. I don't mind it coming out too dull but *too bright*?'

Can you not fix it?

'It's hard to go back in. There's certain things you can do with overglazes. Oh, and transfers.'

I knew nothing about ceramics.

'That cabinet is full of transfers. Look, they're like really posh stickers for clay. You can print anything you want on to the paper. I say *paper* but it's a clear film and the pigment it is made of is basically very fine glass, which means it sinks into the pot, you fire it, and it'll be there for ever. You can bury it in the ground and in a thousand years' time, it will still be there.'

She had this look in her eyes – and I didn't have a fucking clue what she was going on about – but she had this electric look like she had made a groundbreaking discovery, and she was thrilled she could tell someone about it, because then they'd be in on it too.

'Oh, Quest, I forgot to ask if you wanted to be in the show! The studio show. It's not happening until Easter but that should give you enough time to settle in?'

I didn't think I wanted to get involved with that kind of stuff but it was only because it didn't matter any more that it felt so easy to say yes.

I still had a hand around the key in my pocket, so I excused myself and headed for Mo's studio. Sheila made me look forward to the rest of my life. I wanted to make art. I didn't know what, but I wanted to relate to people. I wanted to use my hands. I wanted to get excited about the details. I wanted to stay offline. I wanted to get old. If galleries are where art goes to die, studios are very much alive; and even though the world feels impossible, art is the only reason I'm still here too. Maybe it isn't about the whole world, or the art world, but about this place right now. Sheila's studio, mine. Our small utopia.

Acknowledgements

From the two of us

We would not have been able to write for so many years without our Patreon supporters. Whether you have given us £1 or £100, every donation has given us creative freedom, food, rent, sick pay, travel, and 9 years to build up the courage to write something offline that we can never, ever delete. To our readership, thank you for the conversation, the community, and also for becoming very impressive Google Analytics numbers that we could point to in meetings with publishers and say, *look, people all across the world might buy this weird book.* To whichever Arts Council employee approved the research funding we used to pay inter-viewees and put together the book proposal, knowing we would probably use that money to criticize the very same Arts Council given our track record, we owe you a bevvy. The book simply would not exist otherwise.

Because we had Patreon, we grew a readership; because of that readership, we got invited to lecture at Chelsea College of Art in 2018. When the book proposal came through to Penguin in 2022, Assistant Editor Emmy Yoneda championed it, because Emmy had been a student in the audience at Chelsea when we popped in to talk about The White Pube. We only got a meeting with Penguin because of our agent Milly Reilly, who we met on a train after we had both been invited to a conference in Germany *because* of our writing, *because* of our readership, *because* of our Patreon. These are our dominoes, and Milly's expertise, care and imagination helped us topple the pieces into the shape of *Poor Artists*. Having never formally trained as writers, our editors Josephine Greywoode and fateful Emmy gave us a sharp, rigorous education on the job. They were the very best critics we could have asked for.

In 2022, we got an email from the world's greatest curator, Miguel Amado, asking if there was anything we were working on that he might be able to support. He put us up in Sirius Arts Centre for a month for our first ever residency where we got to work writing, burning through post-it notes, and conducting interviews from the peace and quiet of a potentially haunted basement in Cobh, Ireland. Each person we spoke to in our research gave so much energy to this book. *Poor Artists* is the result of a long domino effect – as is the case with so much art – and our gratitude to each interviewee is infinite.

Thank you to Ali Gitlow at Prestel; to Liz Parsons, Lotte Hall, Jodie Lewis, Ruth Pietroni and Fahad Al-Amoudi at Penguin; Julia Bruce for copy-editing, Francisca Monteiro for text design and Tom Etherington for the perfect cover design. The Game Pube Discord server introduced us to creative non-fiction, and The White Pube Discord server's #what-am-i-thinking-of channel quite literally aided in our research. Please see our publicly available financial accounts on <u>thewhitepube. com</u> if you (or Sangita over in the Art Hospital) want to see line by line how we could just about afford to write this book.

From Gabrielle

I have had Long Covid and POTS since January 2021. For the hundreds of days when my body could only afford to do one thing and I chose to spend that one thing writing this book, I am grateful to be in a relationship with an artist who sacrificed the time he could have spent caring for his own far superior art by caring for me and mine instead. Thank you Michael Lacey for keeping me alive in so many ways.

It is easy to go mad when you are sick and isolated in a small rented house in Liverpool. Thank you to my cousins David, Samantha, Jonny and Simon for the weekly Overwatch games that made me feel like we were back in Nan's house on Friday nights. I spent an undisclosed amount of time playing Apex online with beautiful IGL Liccy, Leicester's greatest artist Gino Attwood, and the singularly talented artist noiamreiss, so all in all, I only went a little bit mad in the end. Voice notes from artist Bella Millroy were better than beta blockers; and the Sick Times group chat with Char, Lauren 'loco' Corelli, and artist Edi McGurk eased me into life as a disabled person more successfully than any doctor could. Thank you Patricia Lacey for keeping the world turning when it felt like it had stopped, and thank you Peter Lacey for knocking on the door like god with dinner in hand. Dr Philip Cumberlidge from the Long Covid clinic was another god. He pulled me out of the red and I could not have written this book if he hadn't. I hope he rests in peace.

I grew up in a house with a Mum who was always making something. Carolyn de la Puente is the reason I am always making something now. My Nan Sheila Kelly is the reason I do not see authority; the artist Anna Hart is the reason I take everybody else so seriously. The scholar Priya Sharma is the reason I'm an anarchist. The filmmaker Holly Márie Parnell is the reason I still let myself care about art being beautiful. EMA, maintenance loans, and the university's hardship fund are the reason I have a degree. Zarina Muhammad is the only person I could have written this with. She is my co-conspirator, co-director, co-brain, co-everything, and this book is proof that we really do finish each other's sentences.

From Zarina

Being a writer in a city as noisy and expensive as London is its own bizarre obstacle course. I wrote my contribution to this book from under the skylight in Exchange, a co-working space in the basement of Somerset House. Thank you Bart Seng Wen Long for telling me about the bursary, and thank you for your help, understanding and kindness. Space is very much a luxury in this city, so I feel incredibly lucky to have this dedicated space to write, think and work.

Thank you to the wolves that raised me: my Mum, my sister, my Akhi fufu. It is an honour to be loved and supported by three women as insane, loud, clever, interesting, cool and kind as you lot. My Dadi, you strange woman, thank you for Quest's surname. It was yours first. Thank you Daoud and Umaya, my favourite artists and my favourite cousins. Thank you to the people I am too shy and coy to name here in print. You might not know who you are, but I do. I'll never say! And that's quite funny and chic, isn't it?

Finally, Gabrielle. I thank my lucky stars that we met because you have taught me almost everything I know that is worth anything at all. I cannot put into words what you mean to me, even though that is quite literally my job.

References

Quest was born in 1994, but she wasn't, because she isn't even real. The artworks referenced are not consistent with her fictional timeline. She saw some things as a baby that didn't even exist back then, and that is fine. Enjoy the references. Goodbye.

Lemon

People museum: Museum of Liverpool, established in 2011.

Boat museum: Liverpool Maritime Museum, established in 1980.

Animal museum: World Museum, Liverpool, established in 1851.

Picture museum: Walker Art Gallery, Liverpool, established in 1877.

Grown-ups doing weird dances: Siobhan Davies Dance's exhibition 'material / rearranged / to / be' at Bluecoat Gallery, Liverpool, 2017.

Animals that hadn't rehearsed and weren't very good: Nam June Paik's exhibition 'Symphony for 20 Rooms' at Den Frie Udstilling, Copenhagen, 2019.

Car crash on the top floor: Moon Kyungwon & Jeon Joonho's exhibition 'News from Nowhere' at Tate Liverpool, 2018–19.

Beach: 'Sun & Sea' performance directed by Rugilė Barzdžiukaitė at the Albany, London, 2022.

Pastel-coloured fog: Anne Veronica Janssens' installation *yellowbluepink* at the Wellcome Collection, London, 2015–16.

Burning sun: Olafur Eliasson's exhibition 'The Weather Project' at Tate Modern, London, 2003–4.

Black rain that stopped as soon as we approached: Random International's installation *Rain Room* at the Barbican Centre, London, 2012.

Walls covered in blue crystals: Roger Hiorns' installation *Seizure* at an empty council flat in London, 2008.

Really strong lights in the shape of alphabetti spaghetti: Maurice Doherty's artwork *I Slept with the Curator to Get This Show*, neon light, 2016.

Room that you had to hum to get into: Adrian Piper's installation *The Humming Room*, 2012; included in the exhibition 'Adrian Piper: A Synthesis of Institutions 1965–2016', The Museum of Modern Art, New York, 2016.

Dark box full of pumpkins and mirrors: Yayoi Kusama's installation *Mirror Room (Pumpkin)*, 1991.

Room full of balloons: Martin Creed's installation *Work No. 200: Half the air in a given space*, 1998.

Exit through the gift shop: Exit Through the Gift Shop, documentary, directed by Banksy, 2010.

Playground slide attached to an upstairs window, pumping visitors out the side of the building: Carsten Höller's exhibition 'Decision' at the Hayward Gallery, London, 2015.

Big sharp silver line sticking out of a roundabout near Quest's house: Gabrielle says she has fully failed to find the name of the artist responsible for the spike sticking out of the roundabout at 53°20'57.4"N 2°52'26.0"W but there are the coordinates if you want to see it for yourself on Google Maps.

Lambanana: Taro Chiezo's artwork *Superlambanana*, sculpture, 1998.

Painting Quest can't look in the eye because it reminds her of the clown that scared her at the fair: The Scream, painting, Edvard Munch, 1893.

The statue that looked exactly like Mum: The Mower, sculpture, William Hamo Thornycroft, 1882–4.

Tuesday-morning playdate for kids at the big museum by the river: The Little Liverpool Gallery at the Museum of Liverpool, established in 2011.

Elmo's Song: Episode 2710, *Sesame Street*, 1990.

Quest's urge to draw on the walls of the living room with crayons: Zarina Muhammad's installation *Christmas Tree* on her mum's living-room wall, London, 1998.

Phrogging

First Thursdays: a monthly promotional event led by Whitechapel Gallery in partnership with *Time Out*, on the first Thursday of every month.

Silent walk: in King's Cross and North Woolwich, London, led by AiR studio, 2016.

Artist's talk: at the Contemporary Art Society, the Subject Specialist Network for contemporary art in the UK, London, established in 1910.

'Quest's next job could be in cyber. She just doesn't know it yet!': UK Government advertisement, 'Fatima's Next Job Could be in Cyber', 2020.

Apichatpong Weerasethakul's multi-channel video installation *Primitive* (2009) in the Tate Modern Tanks, London, 2016.

Max was obsessed with trying to do an Alexis Harding: Alexis Harding's artwork *Slump*, painting, 2004.

A nice Monet exhibition: 'Monet in the 20th Century', Royal Academy of Arts, London, 1999.

Keith Haring's artwork *Radiant Baby*, lithograph, 1993.

Studio Time

Mollie Balshaw's artwork *My studio is on the bus*, painting, 2023.

João Onofre's artwork *Untitled* (Vulture in the Studio), video, 2002.

Ghislaine Leung's Turner Prize installation *Hours*, Towner Gallery, Eastbourne, 2023.

Dawn Kasper's installation *This Could be Something if I Let It*, residency at the Whitney Biennial, New York, 2012.

Tracey Moffatt and Gary Hillberg's artwork *Artist*, video, 1999.

Wendy

Rey Mysterio: Óscar Gutiérrez Rubio aka Rey Mysterio is a wrestler signed to WWE, b. 1974.

Quest's cousins' request for her to do a Michelangelo on the ceiling of Nani's living room: Michelangelo di Lodovico Buonarroti Simoni's fresco *The Creation of Adam* in the Sistine Chapel, Vatican City, 1508–12.

The Undertaker: Mark William Calaway aka 'The Undertaker' is a retired wrestler, b. 1965.

From an interview with Clive Barker on *The South Bank Show*, TV episode, 10 April 1994.

Hellraiser: Clive Barker's novella *The Hellbound Heart*, published by Dark Harvest, 1986.

Candyman: Clive Barker's anthology series 'Books of Blood', published by Sphere Books, 1984–5.

The World's Most Expensive Paintings, documentary directed by Russell England, 2011.

Documentaries about famous fraudsters: Fake or Fortune? documentary series, BBC One, 2011.

Documentaries about famous art thieves: The World's Most Expensive Stolen Paintings, documentary directed by Dominic Gallagher, 2013.

Simon Schama's Power of Art, documentary series, BBC, 2006–8.

Cathy Wilkes' Turner Prize show: Cathy Wilkes' artwork *I Give You All My Money*, mixed media, 2008.

Art language quiz answers:

1. Trompe-l'oeil: French for 'deceives the eye', fancy way of saying optical illusion.

2. Chiaroscuro: Italian for 'light-dark'. Artists in Renaissance times would use extreme contrasts in lighting to make the scenes in their paintings appear more three-dimensional and dramatic.

3. Hegemony: the dominance of one thing over another, also a way of referring to the power a specific thing has, for example, Western hegemony.

4. Imprimatura: paintings can start with an initial wash of a single colour to help the artist sketch the basic composition, and also to make overlying colours pop. Imprimatura is a wash in a terracotta colour.

5. Pentimento: when the ghostly trace of other images or brushstrokes are visible in a painting.

6. Bourgeois: do you own a factory? Do you do the big shop in Waitrose? Do you frequent the opera?

7. Impasto: a painting technique where you lay the paint on so thick and gloopy that your brushstrokes are visible.

8. 'gesso' or 'jesso'? Spelt 'gesso' but pronounced 'jesso'. It's a white, chalky paint mix you use to prime a canvas.

9. How to pronounce 'sfumato'??? It rhymes with the English 'tomato'. It means blending and softening the transition between colours so paint looks hazy.

The Mountain

Boxy black-and-white televisions . . . we think nostalgia matures us: Nam June Paik's artwork *Electronic Superhighway: Continental U.S., Alaska, Hawaii*, installation, 1995.

Boxy black-and-white televisions . . . we think nostalgia matures us: Susan Hiller's artwork *Channels*, installation, 2013.

Mark's mouth, a Lucio Fontana rip-off: Lucio Fontana's artwork *Concetto spaziale 'Attesa'*, canvas, 1960.

Ragnar Kjartansson asks his mother to spit in his face for the sake of video art: Ragnar Kjartansson's artwork *Me and My Mother*, video, 2000–present.

Moody American rock band The National perform their song 'Sorrow' repeatedly for a total of six hours on stage at a gallery in New York: Ragnar Kjartansson & The National, 'A Lot of Sorrow', performance at The Museum of Modern Art PS1, New York, 2013.

She had a frog on her crotch: Maria Lassnig's artwork *Froschkoenigin* (*Frog Princess*), painting, 2000.

A bloated guinea pig in her hand: Maria Lassnig's artwork *Selbst mit Meerschweinchen* (*Self with Guinea Pig*), painting, 2000–2001.

One gun to her head and another aiming directly at the viewer: Maria Lassnig's artwork *You or Me*, painting, 2005.

The cheesy Eat Pray Love *sense:* Elizabeth Gilbert's memoir *Eat, Pray, Love: One Woman's Search for Everything Across Italy, India and Indonesia*, published by Penguin, 2006.

Kara Walker's exhibition at Camden Art Centre, London, 2013–14.

Jumana Manna's exhibition 'A magical substance flows into me' at Chisenhale Gallery, London, 2015.

Chris Kraus' books *Aliens & Anorexia*, published by Semiotext(e), 2000, and *I Love Dick*, published by Semiotext(e), 2006.

'James Baldwin debates William F. Buckley', Cambridge University, 1965.

A video essay using a Craig David deepfake: Zarina Muhammad's artwork *My practice as an eco-system*, moving image, 2016.

A student in the year above announced they were losing their virginity in a live event that people could buy tickets to, only to hoodwink the audience into watching a sexless dance: Clayton Pettet's artwork *Art School Stole My Virginity*, performance, 2013.

Royal Tunbridge Wills

The canvas is attached to a drill and when I pull the trigger . . . the paint spins out . . . it's a psychedelic blur: Damien Hirst's artwork *Spin Paintings*, painting, 1992.

Gerhard Richter's artwork *Forest 3*, painting, 1990.

That's when I remembered to run: 'Jogging', song by Richard Dawson, 2019, from the album *2020*.

I watched the gallery's interns clamber over each other to keep Wills' blood from reaching the walls: Sun Yuan and Peng Yu's artwork *Can't Help Myself*, installation, 2016.

Cilla Black

Blind Date: TV series, produced by London Weekend Television, 1985–2019.

We like Rococo now: Flora Yukhnovich's artwork *Thank Heaven for Little Girls*, 2019.

Artist who felt the need to take out loans, bet on himself, and ultimately ended up bankrupt: '#47 Frederick J. Brown', podcast episode by Kalila Holt for Heavyweight, published by Gimlet Media, 2022.

Get a Job

David Hammons' performance *Bliz-aard Ball Sale*, New York, 1983.

Sophie Calle's artwork *The Hotel, Room 47*, mixed media, 1981.

Linda Aloysius's artwork *The First Painting in History to be Recognized by a Public Museum as Painted by a Working-class Single Mother Artist*, household stains on cotton, 2022.

Jon Edgley's performance *That's a Wrap*, Tesco, Hanover Street, Liverpool, 2019.

David S Gallant's game *I Get This Call Everyday*, 2012.

Who Pays for Art to Happen?

Terrible people with money in need of good press: All the Beauty and the Bloodshed, documentary, directed by Laura Poitras, 2023.

The White Pube's website page 'Successful Funding Application Library', (www.thewhitepube.co.uk/funding-library)
2020.

The Q&A

*They keep letting pubs close down; capitalism has utterly
forced individualism on us:* talk by Mark Fisher, 'All of This
is Temporary', CCI Collective, Rich Mix, London, 2016.

Nicolas Bourriaud's book *Relational Aesthetics*, published by
Les Presses du réel, 1998.

Leo Castelli Gallery, New York, founded in 1957.

Artist Placement Group, arts organization, London, established
in the 1960s.

MAYK, performance-producing organization, Bristol, established in 2011.

Median annual pay for full-time workers was £33,000: Office
for National Statistics report, 'Employee earnings in the UK:
2022', October 2022.

Artists being underpaid subsidizes the rest of the industry:
Industria report, *Structurally F–cked*, published by a-n The
Artists Information Company, 2023.

The head of the Tate is [paid] something like £170,000: Cabinet
Office report, 'Senior officials "high earners" salaries as at 30
September 2021', updated July 2023.

*Talent gets paid the least and the corporate structures around
it leech off us:* 'Geeks, MOPs, and sociopaths in subculture
evolution', article by David Chapman, 2015.

Maslow

Ma Qiusha's artwork *All My Sharpness Comes from Your Hardness*, video, 2011.

Zadie Xa's installation *Child of Magohalmi and the Echos of Creation*, at Walthamstow Library for Art Night UK, London, 2019.

Hannah Quinlan & Rosie Hastings' artwork *Hope, Joy, Youth, Peace, Rest, Life, Dust, Ashes, Waste, Want, Ruin, Despair, Madness, Cunning, Folly, Words, Wigs, Rags, Sheepskin, Plunder, Precedent, Jargon, Gammon and Spinach* at Walthamstow Market for Art Night UK, London, 2019.

Diane Chorley performance at Walthamstow Trades Hall for Art Night UK, London, 2019.

Oscar Murillo's artwork *Letter from America* at Walthamstow Trades Hall for Art Night UK, London, 2019.

John Ongom Big Band performance at Walthamstow Trades Hall for Art Night UK, London, 2019.

War of Attrition

Tiona Nekkia McClodden's artwork *The Brad Johnson Tape, X – On Subjugation*, installation, 2017.

Tiona Nekkia McClodden's artwork *The Brad Johnson Tape [Repair]*, installation, 2022.

Hilde Krohn Huse's film *Hanging in the Woods*, 2014.

Set themselves on fire in a controlled stunt in front of a live audience: Cassils' artwork *Inextinguishable Fire*, performance, 2007–15.

299

Documentary about the Vietnam War: The Inextinguishable Fire, film directed by Harun Farocki, 1969.

Froze their naked body against an ice sculpture of a man's chest for five hours, until their own heat melted the danger away: Cassils' artwork *Tiresias*, performance, 2011.

The No-show

The white cube is where 'the sanctity of the church, the formality of the courtroom, the mystique of the experimental laboratory joins with chic design to produce a unique chamber of aesthetics': Brian O'Doherty's book *Inside the White Cube: The Ideology of the Gallery Space*, published by University of California Press, 1986.

Lubaina Himid's exhibition 'Navigation Charts' at Spike Island, Bristol, 2017.

Bhupen Khakhar's exhibition 'You Can't Please All' at Tate Modern, London, 2016.

Einstein on the Beach, opera, composed by Philip Glass, 1976.

Michaela Yearwood-Dan's exhibition 'The Sweetest Taboo' at Tiwani Contemporary, 2022.

Marijke Vasey's exhibition 'Jeune Creation 71' at Fondation Fiminco, Romainville, France, 2021.

Philip William's artwork *Scratch and Sniff*, painting, 2023.

I was going to build myself an exhibition that no one would ever see: Little Man Gallery, roaming gallery project, run by Gabrielle de la Puente and Michael Lacey, 2016–17.

300

Good Liars

Amalia Ulman's artwork *Excellences and Perfections*, online performance, 2014.

Suzanne Treister's artwork *Fictional Videogame Stills*, mixed media, 1991–2.

William Boyd's book *Nat Tate: An American Artist 1928–1960*, published by Edition Stemmle, 1998.

Piero Manzoni's artwork *Merda d'artista*, mixed media, 1961.

Piero Manzoni's artwork *Corpo d'aria*, mixed media, 1960.

The Real Artists of Beverly Hills

I just have to do a lot of that work to afford to live: 'Working for the Knife', Mitski, from the album *Laurel Hell*, 2022.

'Contemporary Art Daily', website: www.contemporaryart daily.com

Sotheby's, corporation, established in 1744.

K_HOLE, *A Report on Doubt*, published by K_HOLE, 2015.

Robert Crumb's artwork *SHAPE UP!* yoga mat, 2023.

Hyper-Asian art: Babbu the Painter's artwork *Bad Beti Jacket (150CAD)*, apparel, 2017.

David Hockney's artwork *A Bigger Splash*, painting, 1967.

Peter Doig's artwork *Blotter*, painting, 1993

'Abundant production can only result in mediocrity': Calvin Tomkins' book *Marcel Duchamp: The Afternoon Interviews*, published by Badlands Unlimited, 2013

I was jobbing it now: talk by Alexander James Pollard at 'Capitalist Artist Scum #1,' Open School East, London, 2015

Mohammed

Boat painting: Thomas Miles Richardson's artwork, *Lago Maggiore*, painting, 1860.

Valentine

Pulp's song 'Common People', from the album *Different Class*, 1995.

Marina Abramović and Ulay's artwork *The Lovers*, performance, 1988.

Holden Caulfield: J. D. Salinger's book *The Catcher in the Rye*, published by Little, Brown and Company, 1951.

Heathcliff: Emily Brontë's book *Wuthering Heights*, published by Thomas Cautley Newby, 1847.

Citizen Kane, film directed by Orson Welles, 1941.

Graceland: mansion, Memphis, Tennessee; incorporated as a museum in 1982.

'A man's work is nothing but this slow trek to rediscover, through the detours of art, those great and simple images in whose presence his heart first opened': from Albert Camus's essay 'Between Yes and No', 1930s.

Do Not Disturb

Henry Darger's novel *In the Realms of the Unreal*, 1912–72.

Adrian Piper's artwork *Catalysis III*, performance, 1970.

Maria Anwander's artwork *Erased Pictures from Flash Art nr.259*, installation, 2008.

Maria Anwander's artwork *The World's Leading Art Magazine*, installation, 2009.

The Group Crit

Roland Barthes' essay 'The Death of the Author', 1967.

Kurokawa: Ryoichi Kurokawa's exhibition 'unfold' at FACT, Liverpool, 2016.

Thomas Hirschhorn's workshop 'Energy: Yes! Quality: No!', 2013.

Potentially boring: Leonardo da Vinci's artwork *Mona Lisa*, painting, 1503–6.

Uncertainty

Maximum freedom with maximum equality: Ni dieu, ni maître: Une histoire de l'anarchisme, documentary directed by Tancrède Ramonet, 2016.

Tehching Hsieh's artwork *One Year Performance (Time Clock Piece)*, performance, 1980–81.

Tehching Hsieh's artwork *One Year Performance (Rope Piece)*, performance, 1983–4.

Tehching Hsieh's artwork *One Year Performance (Cage Piece)*, performance, 1978–9.

Tehching Hsieh's artwork *One Year Performance (No Art Piece)*, performance, 1985–6.

Tehching Hsieh's artwork *One Year Performance (Outdoor Piece)*, performance, 1981–2.

Lauren Berlant's book *Cruel Optimism*, published by Duke University Press, 2011.

Audre Lorde's essay 'Uses of the Erotic', presented at the Fourth Berkshire Conference on the History of Women, 1978.

Georges Bataille, *Eroticism*, published by Penguin Classics, 2012.

'it was in the black mirror of anarchism that surrealism first recognized itself': from André Breton's article 'The Lighthouse', published in issue 297 of *Le Libertaire*, 1952.

Alberto Giacometti's artwork *No More Play*, sculpture, 1931–2.

Salvador Dalí's artwork *Lobster Telephone*, sculpture, 1938.

Man Ray's artwork *Cadeau*, sculpture, 1921.

phytorio, arts association, Cyprus, established in 2006.

Francis Fukuyama's book *The End of History and the Last Man*, published by Penguin, 1992.

Certainty

Lawrence Abu Hamdan's artwork *Rubber Coated Steel*, video, 2016.

Papo Colo's artwork *Superman 51*, performance, 1977.

Papo Colo's film *La Diferencia (1976–1986)*, produced by Exit Art, 1986.

Sonia Boyce's retrospective at Manchester Art Gallery, 2018.

Agnes Denes' artwork *Wheatfield – A Confrontation: Battery Park Landfill, Downtown Manhattan*, installation, New York, 1982.

Tania Bruguera's artwork *Tatlin's Whisper #5*, live event at Tate Modern's Turbine Hall, 2008.

The Jupiter Residency

Gabrielle de la Puente's game *People of the Salt*, published on Downpour, 2023: www.downpour.games/~gdlp/people-of-the-salt

Liz Crow's artwork *Bedding Out*, performance, 2012–13.

RA Walden & Margaret Ransdell-Green's artwork *x̌ây ithřa: a pledge*, publication, 2021.

Virgina Woolf's essay 'A Room of One's Own,' 1929.

Mia Mingus' essay 'Access Intimacy: The Missing Link', 2011.

Art Hospital

Doris Salcedo's installation *Shibboleth I*, Tate Modern, London, 2007.

Head of security huffing and puffing: in *The Times*, 'Crowds are suffering for their art at Tate Modern', Ben Quinn, 2007.

Christo & Jeanne-Claude's installation *The Umbrellas*, in Japan and USA, 1984–91.

Mary Evans's exhibition 'Cut and Paste' at Tiwani Contemporary, London, 2012.

John Stezaker's exhibition at Whitechapel Gallery, London, 2011.

Female Trouble, film directed by John Waters, 1974.

Giovanni Antonio Canal, aka Canaletto, exhibition 'Venice: Canaletto and His Rivals' at the National Gallery, London, 2010–11.

Christian Marclay's installation *The Clock*, 2010.

A book-style appendix with references, citations, acknowledgements: The White Pube podcast episode 'We got a book deal', 2023.

The ones who pull it off should share those secrets at every opportunity so the rest of us don't feel like shit: The White Pube billboard, *ideas for a new art world 004: people across the creative industries need to declare if they have rich parents who helped them get where they are today*, installation, UK, 2021.

Inquest

Francis Alÿs's artwork *Paradox of Praxis 1 (Sometimes making something leads to nothing)*, performance and video, 1997.

Carlos Martiel's artwork *Plegaria muda* (*Silent Prayer*), performance at Steve Turner Contemporary, Los Angeles, US, 2014.

Aernout Mik's artwork *Communitas*, three-channel moving-image work, 2010.

Lee Lozano: *Dropout Piece*, book by Sarah Lehrer-Graiwer, published by Afterall, 2014.

Nineteenth-century French Painter Gustave Courbet

'Entrust to artists alone the management of their interests': G. Courbet, Moulinet, Stephen Martin, Alexandre Jousse, Roszezench, Trichon, Dalou, Jules Héreau, C. Chabert, H. Dubois, A. Faleynière, Eugène Pottier, Perrin, A. Mouilliard's text, *Manifesto of the Paris Commune's Federation of Artists*, 1871, translated by Jeff Skinner for Red Wedge, 2016.

Spanish Civil War: George Orwell's essay 'Homage to Catalonia', published by Secker and Warburg, 1938.

'From each according to their ability, to each according to their need': Karl Marx's essay 'Critique of the Gotha Programme', 1875.

'The urge for destruction is also a creative urge': Mikhail Bakunin's text 'The Reaction in Germany', 1842.

'We have no fear of ruins, we carry a new world, here in our hearts': Pierre van Passen interview with Buenaventura Durruti, published in the *Toronto Daily Star*, 1936.

'We live in capitalism. Its power seems inescapable. So did the divine right of kings . . .': Ursula K. Le Guin's speech at the National Book Awards, New York, 2014.

The Art King

The Fool: from Pamela Colman Smith's illustration 'Rider-Waite tarot deck', published by the Rider Company, 1909.

F. Scott Fitzgerald's book *The Great Gatsby*, published by Charles Scribner's Sons, 1925.

The Human Centipede (First Sequence), film directed by Tom Six, 2009.

Afterlife

Arnold Böcklin's artwork *The Isle of the Dead*, painting, 1880–1901.

Félix González-Torres' installation *Untitled (Portrait of Ross in L.A.)*, 1991.

Chris Ofili's artwork *No Woman, No Cry*, painting, 1998.

Jonas Dahlberg's proposal 'Memory Wound', 2014.

Lizzy Rose's exhibition 'Things I Have Learned the Hard Way' at Turner Contemporary, LIMBO, Crate & Well Projects in Margate, the ICA in London, and online, 2023.

Mum

Henry Fuseli's artwork *The Nightmare*, painting, 1781.

Sheila

Cassie Thornton's book *The Hologram: Feminist, Peer-to-Peer Health for a Post-Pandemic Future*, published by Pluto Press, 2020.

Horace Pippin's artwork *Holy Mountain I*, painting, 1944.

Linen weaves were found in pharaoh's tombs: Thutmose IV's tomb, tapestry fragments, 1483–11 BCE

Pastor T. L. Barrett & the Youth for Christ Choir's song 'Like a Ship . . . (Without a Sail)', 1971.

Further Thinking

Artists for Palestine's statement 'Art and Occupation: Boycott Zabludowicz', 2015.

Artist coaching with Anna Hart: http://annahart coach.info/

Arch Comics, Janette Parris, 2011–present.

The Price of Everything, documentary directed by Nathaniel Kahn, 2018.

Generation Wealth, documentary directed by Lauren Greenfield, 2018.

Leah Clements, Alice Hattrick & Lizzy Rose's website Access Docs for Artists: https://www.accessdocsforartists.com/about 2018.

'Day Jobs' exhibition at the Blanton Museum of Art, Texas, 2023.

Catalogue for 'Adrian Piper: A Synthesis of Institutions 1965–2016' exhibition, by Christophe Cherix, Cornelia Butler, David Platzker, 2016.

Nina Chua interviewed by Kwong Lee for Workplace Foundation, 2020.

Working Class Creatives Database: https://www.workingclass-creativesdatabase.co.uk

Dürer's Lost Masterpiece: Art and Society at the Dawn of a Global World, Ulinka Rublack, Oxford University Press, 2023.

Hennessy Youngman's YouTube series *Art Thoughtz*, 2010–12.

Mindful Museums, curated by Louise Thompson, 2022–5.